THE DESTINY SERIES

IDENTITY

BOOK 1

3TREES
PUBLISHING

REBECCA D. BENNETT

The Destiny Series ~ IDENTITY ~ Book 1

by Rebecca D. Bennett

Copyright © 2018 by Rebecca Bennett

All rights reserved. This book is protected by the copyright laws of the United States of America. This book may not be copied or reprinted for commercial gain or profit. The use of short quotations or occasional page copying for personal or group study is encouraged. Permission will be granted upon request from Rebecca Bennett. Unless otherwise stated, all biblical quotations are taken from the New International Version. All rights reserved. Any emphasis added to scripture quotations is the author's own.

Scripture quotations marked NIV are taken from the New International Version, © 1973, 1978, 1984, 2011 by Biblica, Inc. Used by permission of Zondervan.

Scripture quotations marked AMP are taken from the Amplified Bible, © 1954, 1958, 1962, 1964, 1965, 1987 by The Lockman Foundation. Used by permission.

Scripture quotations marked MSG are taken from The Message, © 1993, 1994, 1995, 1996, 2000, 2001, 2002 by NavPress. Used by permission.

Scripture quotations marked NLT are taken from the New Living Translation, © 1996 by Tyndale House Publishers, Inc. Used by permission.

ISBN: 978-1-7370190-2-2 (paperback)

ISBN: 978-1-7370190-3-9 (e-book)

Library of Congress Control Number: 2021912029

First Edition Published by SPRING MILL PUBLISHING, Sharpsburg, Maryland 21782 USA

Book 1 Second Edition Published by 3TREES PUBLISHING, LLC, Gulfport, Mississippi 39507 USA

Editing by Laura Rivera-Rexach (laurariverarexach@gmail.com)

Layout by 3TREES PUBLISHING, LLC (3treespublishing@gmail.com

Graphics by Amani Hanson (NoBoxez@Yahoo.com)

DEDICATION

This dedication is made to my Lord and Savior, my best friend and companion above all others. You placed this within me and inspired me to write. You are my Destiny Series. Life with you is an epic journey that never fails to surprise me. Here's to You!

Second honor is given to the one and only individual to whom I've spent the most time with, my only true love, Crispin A. Bennett. I am a better me because he loved me when I couldn't love myself. He saw the good in me when I wasn't even sure if there was good left in me. He showed me that love was worth fighting for and for this, I am eternally in his indebted gratitude. May I be able to love him as unselfishly as he loves me. With all my heart, I love you Crispin.

CONTENTS

INTRODUCTION

THE DESTINY SERIES

Destiny is defined as the power or agency that determines the course of events. Some call it fate, while others call it chance. How does an individual's course of life stay on a determined path in a world of constant change of choices and consequences? For this, we would need to understand a bit of quantum physics, but instead of leading into a discussion on the matter, let's consider a wheel within a wheel.

Two Perspectives

We will approach our study from two perspectives: that of our everyday, earthly lives, and that of God's eternal realm. As human beings, we dwell in both realms, although as redeemed human beings (if you are a Christian), our awareness of our position in the eternal realm grows as we grow in our identities as Christ-ones.

Here is an illustration that you might find helpful. Imagine two wheels—a smaller wheel in the center, a larger wheel surrounding it, each spinning axially from the same axis. The smaller, inner wheel represents our everyday lives. It encompasses the physical and spiritual aspects of our present existence. It exists in space in time. As such, it is finite. The larger wheel represents all of Creation. It is God's world, and it includes everything God ever made: the universe, the seen and unseen realms, the physical and spiritual and beyond. It is infinite.

As the wheels spin, the inner circle turns much faster than the outer circle, at least from our perspective. As we go about our busy lives, our focus naturally tends towards our present circumstances, especially in times of upheaval or elation—the loss of a loved one, a business success or failure, the birth of a child, a car wreck...the myriad of events and our reactions to them that register as exception reporting on the charts of our consciousness.

But in the larger scheme—within the greater wheel surrounding us, what flies off from the inner circle with great force is absorbed by the outer circle with little impact. The outer circle is God's world, and so it reflects God's perspective. It is there that we find lasting peace, calm, and sovereign protection under the wings of the Almighty. We are safe and secure in the greater realm, even as we live in the inner realm. When triumph or tragedy come, our lives will show a greater consequence of the event or trauma than what affects the rest of Creation.

We can mourn the loss of a loved one from the inner-circle perspective, for example, but from the outer circle, God sees no loss, only a change of address, so to speak.

Now, it works the other way too. If something leaves the outer circle and comes to the inner circle, it will have a significant impact on the inner circle. Let us consider what was written in the Gospels: "In the sixth month of Elizabeth's pregnancy, God sent the angel Gabriel to Nazareth, a town in Galilee, to a virgin pledged to be married to a man named Joseph" (Luke 1:26-27). Here, an angel was sent from heaven to earth, and the impact could not have been greater, for the Savior was born as a result of this interaction.

Another illustration of how the circles work together was when Jesus traveled to Bethany after the death of Lazarus. There he was greeted by a distraught group of family and friends, including Mary. At the sight of their grief (and possibly their unbelief) the Bible tell us "Jesus wept" (John 11:35). Eight verses later, he cried out: "Lazarus, come out" (vs. 43). And the dead man came out alive.

We can think of Jesus weeping as an expression of immediate emotion. Surrounded by grief and hopelessness, he broke. From the perspective of the smaller circle, he felt their pain, and perhaps his own. But he did not remain solely in the smaller circle. Within minutes, he connected with the reality that is God's perspective: "If you believe, you will see the glory of God" (vs. 40). And the results were out of this world.

Our lives are real. Our pain, our joy, our giving and caring and losing and weeping...all real from the perspective of the inner circle. But this is not all there is to our existence or our identity. As we probe the depths of our God-given identity, we will understand life from the outer wheel perspective of God's almighty sovereignty and eternal love.

Seed

The force that put your personal destiny in motion is called seed. You were formed in your mother's womb. You are a seed within a seed bearer. There is no faith required for seed to grow. If a seed is placed in the right environment, given the proper conditions, it will grow. It is the law of nature, one that I refer to as The Kingdom Principle. Seeds are made to grow to maturity in the land and produce a harvest.

Within you is a will to live. You are a design in the physical dimension made up of flesh, bone, organs, and blood. You are also a spiritual being containing mind, will and emotions. You represent a wheel within a wheel. As you live and grow, you continue to occupy time and space. You were a seed in a conducive environment to grow. Then you were separated and grew into a mature being capable of producing seed. The cycle continues.

The land partners with us to produce seed. What do I mean by "partner"? The Creation around us (I refer to as *land*) serves a purpose. It was created to provide for creatures of the earth. The land follows the same Kingdom Principle that we do regarding the seed. The land and waters are meant to produce by recycling the air we breathe, providing food and water—resources for our livelihood and habitation. Moreover, it is from the land, our gifts and talents, that we have the ability to produce a wage or create wealth that leaves behind a legacy of blessing through our birthright.

I cannot create gold, but if I mine the gold from the land, I now possess a resource of commodity. The land and I have teamed the resources, creating an ability to use the gold for tools, trade the gold for something else, or set it aside to grow in wealth. I cannot make vegetables, yet I can plant seed and wait for them to produce. Once they produce, I can set aside seed for the next planting. I can also sell some of the produce, store some of it, and eat it from the harvest. This is another Kingdom Principle that I refer to as The Livelihood.

Kingdom Principle

What is a Kingdom Principle? A Kingdom Principle is when you follow a pattern in scripture that reoccurs before Mosaic Law, then continues throughout the ages of the Mosaic Law and is also demonstrated in the New Testament through the teaching of Jesus Christ. A Kingdom Principle is a law of God's heart for his Creation. In order to explain what I mean, go with me on a stroll in the Garden of Eden before the fall of mankind.

God placed man in the center of the Garden of Eden. It doesn't say that God built for them a home or cooked them dinner, but he did plant a garden with food, water, and gold. Even as God saw that it was not good for man to be alone, he provided a mate. Because the scriptures say that God knows a need before we ever think it, we can conclude that he knew Adam and Eve would need basic necessities to live and procreate. Therefore, everything they would require for survival was provided on earth. God used the resources of what the earth yielded to create Adam from the dust and Eve from the rib of Adam. This is where the Kingdom Principles of the seed, land and livelihood originate—with the sower and the reaper or giver and the receiver.

God's directives during creation establish a blueprint of destiny. Genesis 1:20-22 tells the water creatures and the birds to be fruitful and increase in number. Then in verse 24, God tells the land to produce living creatures according to its kinds. Verse 26 is where he declares that man should be made in his likeness to rule over all the creatures of the earth. Then in verse 27, he tells man to be fruitful and increase in number (seed), fill the earth, and subdue it (take care of it and occupy). Genesis 1:29-30 is where God gives every seed-bearing plant containing fruit and seed to man for food, and every green plant to animals for food. It was the law of the land to supply food and shelter for all created things. This is a depiction of the wheel within a wheel relationship between God and the land, God and man, man and seed, man and land. Man's prosperity or livelihood is based out of his obedience to do as God says regarding the seed and land whilst the land obeys God to produce on behalf of man. When the land does not follow the Kingdom Principle, it is cursed. Example: Jesus passed by the fig tree and it was bare. When he passed by again it was still bare, so Jesus cursed the fig tree. We are supposed to cut off the roots to that which does not produce fruit.

It was not the intention of God for man to work the ground in toil or to experience pain in childbearing. This was the consequence of wrong choices that led to disobedience. God had to cut Adam and Eve off from the Tree of Life because they were cursed. The pattern of this Kingdom Principle remains true throughout. Such examples of the Old Testament are found in the story of Job, Abraham, Isaac, Jacob, David, and Solomon. In the New Testament, you will need to study the life of Jesus and his disciples. The seed of Jesus is represented by those who believe he is the Messiah. He made a livelihood from carpentry, and yet his destiny as a man provided so much more.

When Jesus gained the keys to the kingdom through his death and resurrection, he made copies of those keys which he placed inside the spirit of all who believe upon him and receive his spirit. This is where the larger wheel comes in; the 'unseen', God and the 'seen on earth', Jesus. Our life is lived in the smaller wheel, at the center of Kingdom destiny, glory to glory.

In order to fill the earth and subdue it, according to God's blueprint, we must first understand Kingdom Principles. I will cover more of these as we journey through *The Destiny Series*, but the seed, land, and livelihood are part of our destiny that must be explored as we begin to build a foundation of our Identity in Christ. As we delve into different types of identifiers and how you identify yourself in them, it will be important to evaluate and eliminate identifiers that oppose what God says about you and adopt the truth for your life, so you'll prosper and produce in your destiny. *The Destiny Series* is designed to train and equip you to discover your identity, purpose, and authority in order to align with God's blueprint for your life in him.

How To Use This Book

The first edition of this book was designed as a 11-week course. Each chapter representing a week of study, introducing a new lesson, a memory verse and five daily assignments. Each daily assignment contains a devotional, a Bible reading, a brief writing exercise and a daily challenge. The second edition broke the book down into two pieces; the book only consisting of the Chapter overviews, and the study guide containing the personal study and application.

The Destiny Series is formulated to complement individual teaching and ministerial styles. Use it as a resource, a guide, or a reference.

Journey toward your IDENTITY in any of these variations:

- Read the chapter book
- Get the study guide for personal development
- Do the daily study
- Read as a personal devotional
- Read with your book club
- Form a-study group; facilitate a class at home, work, school, church and/or through your ministry

Get into it any way you can!

Tools Needed:

- Bible
- Pen/Pencil, Highlighter
- Bible Concordance (available via book or apps)
- Dictionary (if needed)
- Email me if you have questions about a point or meaning at rebeccadbennett.tds@gmail.com
- Access to Internet

PERSONAL

IDENTITY

1

PHYSICAL IDENTITY

I have always been a student of human identity—who we are as beings created in the image of God, and who we are as beings redeemed by the ongoing work of Holy Spirit through the blood covenant of Jesus Christ.

Although I had written extensively on the subject of identity in the past, deeper revelations have come into my heart from the simplest of sources: an online dictionary. As I searched the word _identity_, my heart echoed the same thought over and over: _Lord, I want to really understand the full realm of identity and what that means to you._

Because of my yearning, I allowed the Holy Spirit to bring deeper curiosity and understanding into my heart. As my search intensified, what I found captivated me. It is this revelation that I am sharing in this study.

Defining Identity

We can define identity in five ways.

1. The state or fact of remaining the same

Although the world around me changes, I remain a human being. I am still a mammal. I am still female. My DNA stays the same (for the most part), as do my fingerprints, eye pattern and blood type.

What happens if a nurse gives you the wrong blood type in a transfusion? You have a severe reaction, and you die instantly. Likewise, our eye pattern is unique to us and can be used to verify our identity. I can change the appearance of my face in plastic surgery, but unless I get a new eye implanted, my eye will remain the same.

These and other aspects of my identity remain the same under varying conditions.

2. The instance or point of sameness or likeness

In this definition of identity, the likeness appears remarkably similar, but they have unique identities. This is best revealed in cases of mistaken identity. Have you ever been mistaken for another person? Perhaps you have the facial features or body shape that reminds people of someone else. Such similarities can cause instant connection, even though the two people who share physical traits are actually vastly different. Even identical twins are not 100 percent the same. Each is unique.

3. The state or fact of being the one described

If I were in front of you, you might describe me as a "short lady with intense brown eyes and styled hair."

There are descriptions that we use to identify others. We've heard the old idiom: "If it looks like a duck, if it walks like a duck, if it quacks like a duck, it's probably a duck...until you see a goose."

Identity is not always visual. Are you capable of identifying the sound of a loved one in a busy shopping mall or a friend's laugh in a crowded restaurant? Yes, you can.

Imagine a litter of newborn kittens whose eyes are still sealed shut. They can't see, but they can sniff around and smell their mama. They just nudge right up to her. They know exactly who their mama is. Why is this? They begin to use their five senses to be able to identify her.

A visually impaired individual might use their hands. They can trace your face and become fully able to identify you. Or perhaps they will learn your voice.

If a person walks toward us from far away, we can subconsciously determine whether it's a son, a daughter, a spouse, a sister, or a brother just by the way they move—their gait.

We make decisions about our identity through our experience.

4. The condition of being oneself and not another; an exact likeness in nature or qualities

Each person has a specific set of interests, decisions and experiences that express their identity. We create a likeness or nature in our associations, perhaps through a school, a profession, or a hobby. If I'm an accountant, I might enjoy the company of other accountants. If my father was a teacher, my mama was a teacher and my brother was a teacher, chances are I grew up playing school all the time and I might seriously consider becoming a teacher someday.

We broaden our identity through acceptance, and we narrow our identity through rejection. Our identity is shaped through these decisions. This is important. If you want to overcome an area in which you have pre-judged and cannot seem to change your mind, broaden your definition of acceptance through your identity. It begins with us.

Perhaps exercise is something you have trouble prioritizing. So you start by broadening your acceptance that it is important. You might say to yourself, "I know I need to exercise. I recognize that a sedentary lifestyle is not healthy. I know I'm not a triathlete, and I'm not going to run 20 miles a day. But I am going to seek out enough exercise that it expands my health."

Make room for new thinking through acceptance. Be mindful to embrace the fact that we are all different and have things that interest us in different ways. Lay aside thought patterns and attitudes that don't serve you well. Use your authority to be who you were created to be and expand your identity to allow others to be who they've been created to be.

5. An exact likeness in nature or qualities, and sometimes disturbed

Our experiences influence how we respond to similar circumstances, and this becomes a part of our identity.

Imagine you experienced a car wreck in which you were rear-ended. Two years later, you're rear-ended again. Six months after that, you're rear-ended for the third time. It's not hard to understand that every time you look in that rear-view mirror after that, you're guarded. If a car behind you seems to be approaching quickly, you are now more likely to prepare for impact.

For another example, consider being a small child in the first car wreck. Now, if your mother was in the driver's seat and she had an extremely emotional response, including a commotion outside of the vehicle between her and the other driver, you might form a response. You could become afraid for your mother.

Now, fast forward to when you are 16 years old. You are learning to drive, and you get rear-ended. You could become emotionally disturbed because you are expecting a huge fight outside the vehicle. So you get out of the car and become combative, even though you are unprovoked. Your reaction is fueled by what is happening *within* you, not *without* you. Your memory has changed you.

Conversely, your memory could have been a pleasant one. Your mother could have exited the car calmly, exchanged information with the other driver, accepted their apology and returned in a relaxed mood. From that experience, your reaction to your first traffic accident would be much more pleasant.

Not only must we understand how our experiences influence our behavior, but we must also be mindful of how our reactions affect those who are observing us. There are always consequences to our actions—direct and indirect.

Maslow's Hierarchy of Needs

When people experience deep trauma, it creates a false identity within them, and so it has to be corrected for them to function well in mainstream life. This is important because we have to deal with the emotional-response components of an individual before we can ever expect them to discover and develop their full personality as redeemed individuals in Christ.

Maslow's hierarchy of needs is a convenient tool to identify and prioritize basic human needs leading to what is termed "self-actualization," a condition synonymous with full, healthy identity.

FIGURE 1- Maslow's Hierarchy of Needs

Physiological

Our inner needs are as essential to identity as breathing is to life, as food, water, and sleep are to the body. What happens if we don't have enough sleep? We become sleep-deprived and irritable. Eventually, our immune system begins to break down. Our homeostasis—the equilibrium of our body's functions and wellness—is thrown out of balance.

Our body has to be functioning properly to have this physiological need met. If our kidneys shut down, do we have a healthy life? Of course not. We need to give this condition our immediate attention. Whatever is causing the problem must be fixed because it is altering the well-being of the entire body.

In the same way, the wellbeing of our identity is challenged by our experiences and the alternate realities formed around them. Negative experiences affect us powerfully and change us in unseen ways.

If we had a loving, secure home, we are probably secure in our identity at some level. On the other hand, if we were rejected, kicked around, and treated like trash, we probably don't have a strong healthy sense of identity. This is because our primary psychological needs were neglected, even abused.

Consider being a teenage mother and having to care for an infant when your peers are going to high school dances. How would you view life and social standing after such an experience?

Think of being left in a cold bedroom for weeks with no food. What would develop in place of your sense of security? Would you grow up stealing to stay fed? Or would you hide food in your basement? Become miserly?

If you were taunted by bullies throughout childhood, would you finally emerge angry and aggressive? Or meek and oppressed?

All of these negative experiences can be detrimental to a healthy spiritual identity, one that is true to the Word of God.

Positive experiences, on the other hand, can affect us just as powerfully in a good way. A childhood of encouragement, validation and security builds a healthy identity that can lead to good performance reviews in our occupations, running a successful corporation and building loving interpersonal relationships. Success breeds success. This is why it is essential that we help people by first getting them on a level playing field. They need a fighting chance. They need an identity they can build on.

Safety

When we are caring for someone who has experienced extreme trauma, no matter whether that trauma was physical, emotional, or psychological, we begin by providing a safe, secure environment. We have to demonstrate a quiet, stress-free place that meets their basic needs while allowing for their physical condition to unwind. Initially, they may sleep for weeks and wake up only when they're hungry or need the bathroom. If they're strung out on drugs, they must be weaned off slowly to avoid triggering their body into shock or death.

But whatever the case, their immediate need is safety. They need to believe that their abuser is not returning for them. They need to know they can trust someone. To establish this trust, you act in a nonjudgmental way, supplying nourishment, warmth, and other attributes of a loving home. The goal is to provide an environment rich in safety and security in order to promote a relationship of trust.

Love and Belonging

A vital component of this nurturing environment is love and belonging. If I'm providing for someone's physiological needs and safety, but I don't have love for that person, they will not experience the full nurturing that they need for a healthy identity.

Love and belonging appear in many forms, including friendship, family, and interpersonal intimacy. Intimacy is not always sexual; it is present when touch and relationship are formed in mutual trust. Touch is important in expressing love.

Esteem

Without experiencing the healing effects of love and belonging, it is nearly impossible for a person to believe they have value. If a person has the first three conditions of Maslow's hierarchy—safety, physiological, love and belonging—but does not build esteem, they will see themselves small, dependent, deriving at no real sense of purpose. The low-esteemed become dependent on others to provide essential needs and may demonstrate this through a lack of personal hygiene, withdrawing or failing to set or achieve goals. They do not regard others around them or things others may value. A child who has esteem issues may repeatedly destroy another child's toys as well as their own.

Self-Actualization

Becoming fully ourselves includes the development of morality, expressions of creativity, spontaneity, problem-solving and ultimately a sense of fulfillment in whatever we choose to do with our lives.

In this phase, our prejudices—judgmental strongholds that formed when we were young—lose their power. Our parents expressed opinions that we observed and adopted. As we grow, we formulate our identity through our social environment, our safety and security, and our experiences. But when we reach self-actualization, we begin to put into motion the spiritual qualities of the Holy Spirit which reshapes our identity. We ask questions and make different judgments than those displayed to us in childhood.

The Lord took me on this path a couple of years ago. He was teaching me something, and I said, "I don't think I believe that."

He responded, "I'm going to show you why this is the way that it is. You can believe me if you want. I'm just trying to teach you."

And so I allowed him to change my mind. As I looked at my beliefs from his perspective and allowed him to ask me questions, I realized I did not have the merit of truth behind my conclusions. But I was up for the challenge, and it taught me that I didn't know everything. It was good to be humbled again before him. He showed me wrong beliefs and judgments in my heart, and he exposed the areas of my life that still needed developing. They had not been nurtured well, and thus they needed his care.

Identity Element

Our identity is comprised of fundamental elements from key relationships in our lives. These areas include the most intimate: marriage, friendship, and family. Within these realms, we have a different relationship with each person in our lives. We can't treat one person the same as another because each person has their own identity, and their identities contribute to our identity.

As the body of Christ, we were designed independently of one another so that we can function well together. We have varying gifts, unique personalities and diverse physical traits that make up our piece of the body of Christ. Yet we are all the same body with Christ, puzzle pieces that form the whole picture, united along the edges of our individual characteristics.

I will build my church, and the gates of Hades will not overcome it.

Matthew 16:18

When you come into your identity in Christ, you become part of a functioning unit formed like Maslow's hierarchy. You become part of a body. This is the goal of forming our identity. This is why we work to ensure the essentials are present in our prayer, our words, and our worship, all flowing into the river of our identity. Safety flows into our relationships and intimacy. We build unified teams based on an active prayer life with other prayer warriors. We become comrades. Like soldiers in combat, we vow to leave no one behind, and we will endanger ourselves to retrieve a fallen teammate. No matter what, we finish the assignment, accomplishing the mission in the Spirit of God's oneness. *We few, we happy few, we band of brothers and sisters.*

So many people get off track of their mission because they get offended or they can't get along with somebody. One of the enemy's favorite tactics is to divide and conquer. Whatever comes between us, comes against us. Yes, it can feel good to go off on your own, at least, at first. But sooner or later, you'll be alone, and suddenly, the stakes will be higher than you can manage.

Our map is the Word with the leading of Holy Spirit. We are one body. We choose to work in partnership with one another. Do the kidneys need to keep track of what the lungs are doing? No, they each pay attention to their own function. But when the lungs fall ill, the kidneys are affected. It is naive to think that what you do doesn't have an impact on the body around you. We are all connected in spirit. While there are qualifications for God's assignments, there is no qualification for being a spiritual creation. You simply are. And your contribution to that unseen environment—good or bad, pure or polluted—is related to who you are in Christ.

We need to understand who we are because we have a specific assignment to fulfill. Every cell that is developed and formed in our bodies has a specific function. There's not one thing that goes wasted. Even your fat serves a purpose. (OK, I get it. We don't necessarily like it, but a proportional amount serves a purpose.)

> For even as the body is one and yet has many members, and all
> the members of the body, though they are many, are one body, so
> also is Christ.

> I Corinthians 12:12 NASB

Even though there are many of us, there is ultimately only one of us: the body of Christ, redeemed by his blood, healed by his ascension, and united by his Spirit.

Unity

We are one body in Christ, but we have different identities, gifts and talents, and purposes. Unity is seen as we all work toward the goal of bringing the Kingdom of Heaven here on the earth, so that Jesus can come back for a spotless bride. But in that unity, my role is different from other people's roles. I may wish I had some of the abilities or strengths that others have, but I've learned to embrace the part that God gave me. (Of course, if I'm open and I steward the gifts he's given me, he may choose to give me more. It is imperative that I work with what he has given me.)

I have come to understand that I am who I am, and I see things the way I see them. I can embrace the identity the Lord has placed within me. But of course, I am far from perfect—though I'm trying, just as we all are—and so I have learned to partner with a brother or sister. Because their gifts are unique from mine, they can help make me stronger where I am weak. Likewise, I can help them realize areas where they are weak. The key is to be teachable. We do not need to change who we are but be able to grow. We teach others to grow through love and are careful not to offend.

Others may possess the sight to see what I do not. Often, they are sensing only a part—their part. When we join our perspectives in unity, then the whole matter comes clearer into view, equipping us to pray effectively.

That's how the body of Christ works. That's how we get help. That's how we unite.

> *For by one Spirit we were all baptized into one body, whether Jews or Greeks, whether slaves or free, and we were all made to drink of one Spirit.*

I Corinthians 12:13 NASB

When we accept Christ, the old things pass away, and we become brand new. We literally shed our old mindsets, decisions and judgments that formed a false identity. Our old ways go, and we are transformed into a new identity.

Our body gives us our authority on earth. That's why Jesus had to come in the form of a man. He had to put on his man suit. But when you become a Christ- one, you need to shed that skin. Your spirit man needs to come forward and be a part of everything that you do. Your spirit's identity was formed before the foundation of the world.

> *Before I formed you in the womb I knew you, before you were born I set you apart.*

Jeremiah 1:5

The identity that God placed in you needs to come forward because it has gifts, talents and resources that have not been tapped into yet. Maybe you've tapped into some of them, but it's been benefiting the world, not Christ. When you tap into the full access of your spirit man, you can unleash the fullness of who you are in Christ Jesus to fulfill the supernatural things of the Father.

When we know our identity—not who the world teaches us that we are, but who our Father says we are—things change. Atmospheres change. Dimensions shift. Everything we do is transformed because we are operating through our spirit man as one with Christ. We are now operating in his Kingdom.

> *Therefore, if anyone is in Christ, he is a new creature; the old things passed away; behold, new things have come.*

2 Corinthians 5:17 NASB

Being born again is a remarkable transformation; it's a rebirth. How does that happen? Nicodemus asked Jesus how this could be. Could he go back into his mother's womb? No. Rather, we are shedding that man skin and are awakened in the spirit to be that son or daughter of God that was in his mind before the foundation of the world.

If you want to think of yourself as a superhero, go right ahead, because you are.

If we look at a caterpillar, do we say, "Look at that butterfly?" No. It's a caterpillar. The same is true of our old skin. That flesh is dying. We are that caterpillar. We bear the image of an identity that has been established through the world's eyes, not through godly eyes.

In Christ, metamorphosis happens in us. We may not see the change in its entirety, but change is coming, a complex evolution from the person formed by sin to the person formed in spirit through love's redemption. "Christ in you, the hope of glory" (Colossians 1:27).

If you were to talk to someone who regularly sees in the spirit, they might comment about your aura—the energy surrounding you. Well, the truth is, our aura changes as we become a Christ-one. And it shows how developed you are in aligning your word with God's Word. The further along you go with Christ, and the deeper you are in relationship with Christ's body, the brighter and stronger your aura becomes.

It's unmistakable to those who see in the spirit. Indeed, all those around you will sense it in some way. You can be in the midst of ten thousand people, and if you are a steward of your relationship with Christ, his light will project to them. They may not all see it, but they will all respond to it in some way. They will know you in a crowd. We are marked. Jesus is our mark.

We have been transformed, and they're seeing our butterflies. We can ask the Lord to show it to us. This is how we learn to feel the spirits of others, recognizing someone before we see them.

Even though we're the butterfly, we are constantly changing, growing, and getting stronger. We are forever developing. That's what healthy, growing things do.

> *And we all, who with unveiled faces contemplate the Lord's glory,*
> *are being transformed into his image with ever-increasing glory,*
> *which comes from the Lord, who is the Spirit.*

> 2 Corinthians 3:18

In this Destiny Series, we're going to start with Identity—taking a closer look at ourselves. It is not intended to take the focus off of Christ, but rather we are opening the door for Christ to do a greater work within us. We want to molt that skin. Consider your present circumstances as your cocoon right now. I know you're already butterflies, but we're cocooning to take inventory, to get a better footing for where we're going. In the days to come, the demand for us as Christ-ones is going to be brighter. There are going to be many new believers. They're going to need people who know who they are in Christ, who know their purpose, who know their authority and who can teach them how to walk well. Allow them the opportunity to cocoon with you while they take personal inventory to create healthy change in their identity.

Our transformation looks like this:

- I'm not loved.   *Yes*, you are loved.
- I'm not worthy.   *Yes*, you are worthy.
- I'm not good enough. *Yes*, you are good enough.

You were chosen before the foundations of the world. Your gifts and callings are forever and ever! Amen.

Make sure that your heart is steady after Jesus. Put in the practice of your daily prayer, worship, and Bible reading. Take time for your devotion. Get into your Word and study. Worship and spend time with God.

This journey through identity will help you heal from false beliefs and generational strongholds. You will learn your redemptive gifts. You will get wisdom for healthy conflict resolution. You will start from where you are and take inventory of where you've been, asking these things:

- What things you should shed?
- What ideas need development?
- Who are you, really?
- Where are you in this season?
- What do you want to do in the seasons to come?
- What is your heart crying to do?

Your commitment to this in-depth process is going to bring you through. The blessings are going to come through the messianic roots and the role you play in restoring the Kingdom on Earth. You're going to learn exactly what it means in the Word. You're going to see the blessings and promises that have come forward, not only through the Word, but also through your generational line. These will show who you are and the role you fulfill.

Your generational line has a purpose. We don't set that aside. We look into it and bring it forward into the new identity. You may not know what was in your generational line, but the Lord can tell you. The Lord can pull up unanswered prayers from generations before. You can bring them into the present because you stepped into that generational identity. There will also be some elements of generational identity that you will need to lay down.

The Law was established to use as a measure for what was holy and acceptable to God, a measure of good and evil. Jesus came to fulfill the Law. We live fully in Jesus our Messiah, not by the Law. Yet as believers, we do not discard the Law any more than Jesus discarded us in our sins as breakers of the Law.

Now, our hope of life is found in him, and he is life. Let us now rise to the occasion, discovering the fullness of all he has for us, of all he created us to be when he first surveyed the abyss and spoke these words over the new creation: "Let there be...!"

2

SPIRITUAL INTEGRITY

Previously, we reviewed the cracks and criticisms in our hearts that keep us from the fullness of God. These are soulish issues that need to be dealt with. We have to work them out and subdue them. We do this by resisting that urge to do the things of the natural and remembering to step into the spirit realm—the spiritual aspects of life. When we leave open doors, we have cracks in our spiritual integrity. We begin to be compromised, and we suffer the consequences.

For example, a dam protects the land from washout, but it's also used for water conservation. If a dam gets a small crack in it, it is detrimental to the structure, regardless of how grand and strong it appears. Eventually, that crack, untreated, will spread and destroy the dam and the land it was built to protect.

The same thing happens in our soul when we allow a compromise in righteousness to occur that opens doors to our spirit-man. We have to go back and close doors and seal cracks that have been created. Sometimes we created these doors before we knew Christ; other times we opened doors after we knew Christ.

We walk out our salvation every day. God's mercies never come to an end; they are new every morning. Knowing this gives us opportunity to reflect. _I was struggling in this area yesterday. I've just created an open door, so I need to take a moment to deal with that issue before the opening gets any wider._ Without this awareness, the enemy will come in to torment you, and he'll continue because now he's got the legal right to aggravate the wound.

God created everything perfect in his likeness and image. This includes us. We have to protect what God is doing deep within our hearts because he's creating us in a new likeness and image in him. When we accept him as our Savior, there's a period of time when we're still cocooning, morphing into a beautiful butterfly. We're going through a transition, recognizing when our flesh is battling our inner man, understanding the stakes of the battle, and choosing rightly to align our hearts with his heart.

Our encounters with Jesus change us. *I melted at the altar, just undone. I'm not the same.* Our lives change. Our old hangouts and friendships don't fit us anymore. We start telling our friends about Jesus and hanging out with them until they either get saved or they move on without us.

Our growth with Christ is an unstable, beautiful period. It feels good, clean, and new. As we come out of that cocoon and we understand who we are, we stand on the Word and learn to pray. We find supportive believers to help us when we struggle. They recognize that we're newbies and they say to us: "If you need anything, you call me. If you're struggling with something, you call me. Come to my house; we'll hang out. You want to go out? You want to go get a meal? Call me."

This is how we acclimate to our new being as we become a strong wall, a defense in our spirit-man. We are weak, but God is strong. We have to expose and strengthen our weak areas. The more we fill ourselves with Jesus, the stronger we become and the more we can take care of those open doors on our own.

The key to everything, however, is integrity. Our redemption, our spiritual life, our ministry, and our relationship with God are all governed by integrity.

Integrity is "the adherence to moral and ethical principles; soundness of moral character; honesty."

Honesty doesn't seem to exist much these days. There was a time when you could shake a person's hand and it was as good as their word. It was a deal. You didn't need a contract or attorneys. There were still dishonest people in the world, but there were many more honest ones. People had more integrity than they do now. Today, it's much harder to find people of integrity.

Having the spirit of Jesus, integrity should be at the core of who we are. When we opt to not show up at a place where we committed to being, it's important to be truthful and have enough integrity to own our decision. Why are you not there? Is it because you just don't want to be bothered with it right now? Maybe you don't feel good. Maybe you just don't want to. It's OK to just say: "I just really don't want to go anywhere tonight. I just feel like taking time off. I've been running 90 miles an hour and I haven't had a day off in three weeks. I want to honor the Lord and take a day of rest."

Your honesty is valid. Nobody worthwhile is going to judge you for expressing your limitations and need for rest. Do you realize your honesty comes across a lot better than a flimsy excuse? When I receive a veiled excuse, I cringe inside, because I wish they would just tell me the truth.

What are the excuses we tell ourselves? If we want to lose 10 pounds, are we going to do it or are we going to make excuses about why we are not doing it?

It's the same with our relationship with God. People lie to God all the time. I've done it and not even realized it. But then it hits me: What did I just say? Lord, I repent! Forgive me.

We can be honest with God. We're not fooling him. Really, we are only fooling ourselves. We need to be honest with ourselves and honest with others. The world makes it so easy to make excuses, but as believers in Christ, everything we do should be done rightly and with excellence. We are examples of what a *Christ-one* should be. When we lie, we can be sure our sins will find us out.

Scripture is clear about lying:

Do not steal. Do not lie. Do not deceive one another.

Leviticus 19:11

The Lord detests lying lips, but he delights in people who are trustworthy.

Proverbs 12:22

Do not lie to each other, since you have taken off your old self with its practices.

Colossians 3:9

That's pretty straightforward. (If anyone sees any ambiguity in these verses, feel free to contact me at the email in the back of this book.)

We trained our children in honesty at an early age. When one of our kids would tell me a half-truth, I'd respond: "Do you realize you just lied to me?" Then I'd point out the inconsistencies in their words. People often believe that little omissions or half-truths aren't lies. But what is dishonesty? It is not being truthful. What is not truthful? It is conveying something other than the whole truth. When we let others believe a lie, we are complicit in their false sense of reality.

Sometimes we lie because we don't want to hurt another person's feelings. But to lie is sin, and it compromises our spiritual integrity. The truth is, we care less about their feelings and more about sparing ourselves the burden of dealing with their hurt feelings.

My granddaddy used to say "You've got your name, and that goes with you for all your life. Once you lose your name, it's gone."

Everything we do and say is tied back to our name. What do you want your name to represent? We've become Christ-ones. We represent a different name. God is not a man that he should lie. There's no dishonesty in him whatsoever. He is full force in all integrity — a state of being whole, entire, and undiminished.

For instance, to preserve the integrity of an empire means to keep it whole. When it breaks off piece by piece by piece, it is beginning to crumble and weaken, soon to be overtaken. Wholeness is a vital part of integrity. Any organization is as strong as its unity and as weak as its division. Integrity is strongest when it is integral to the organization.

As the body of Christ, we represent integrity. Yet we hear of churches kicking people out, separating from certain leaders and creating discord.

This can be the attack of the enemy, or it can be the work of the Lord to achieve unity through his Spirit.

Conflict within the body of Christ increases when key issues don't get addressed promptly and thoroughly. People prefer to turn and look the other way, refusing to acknowledge sin and how it's undermining the body of Christ. Yes, it's not easy to confront other people. The most difficult part is facing our own integrity issues before addressing the same on others. Judgment begins at home.

There was a music minister in our church who sexually harassed several women. Yet he wasn't removed right away. Instead, leadership gave him the opportunity to correct his behavior and come under the authority of Christ. When he refused, he was asked to leave. In hindsight, allowing him to stay for that season only exacerbated the damage his sin had done.

Now, being tolerant and patient is part of God's love. We all can have bad days or be blind to key faults that become all too apparent at the worst possible time. We deserve the opportunity to face our issues, yield our hearts to the Lord and say "Lord, OK, I didn't like the way I responded to that. Work on me. Do some heart surgery."

What is redemption other than heart surgery? It's part of the process. So is keeping the organization in an unimpaired, perfect condition. Consider the integrity of a ship's hull. Once a breach is found, it must be repaired, otherwise the ship is at risk of sinking. An organization is the same. It rises or falls on the integrity of its people.

Remember, we're not striving for perfection; we are striving for excellence. That means dealing with critical issues as circumstances warrant. A drunk friend at a party is one thing. We can see that she gets home alright and find her in the coming days with scriptures and prayer. A drunk in a hospital operating room, however, is an entirely different matter.

Christ-ones

Whatever we do, we are to do it well because we represent Jesus. Those around us may not even know our names, but if we do it right—following the Holy Spirit—God will be remembered forever. Pursuit of God trumps anything we might seek for ourselves: money, fame, recognition, even validation.

Does that mean we don't have our own personalities and dispositions that contribute to the body of Christ? Of course, we do. God made us that way. He likes diversity. (If you don't believe it, count the flowers in a mountain meadow sometime.)

Each of us is needed. Each of us is valuable. Whether we are fast or slow, genius or average, strong or weak, fun, or serious, each of us has a unique role to play. We are all gems in the hands of the master jeweler. We are constantly on display as his handiwork.

Ministry taught me to stretch myself, causing my weaknesses to strengthen. I realized that part of ministering to people is living in a glass house. Sometimes, it feels as if the walls are a magnifying glass. Everything I do, everything my family does, is observed, amplified, and broadcast to the world at large.

We all experience this, whether we realize it or not. The minute that you confess Jesus as your personal savior, two things happen. His light shines within you, and you get noticed. People are going to realize there's something different about you. Some are going to like it; some are going to hate it, and all will be curious about it. In all this, remember who you represent and what is at stake—no less than the world and all that is in it.

> *This is the judgment, that the Light has come into the world, and men loved the darkness rather than the Light, for their deeds were evil.*

> John 3:19 NASB

God's Word

The enemy uses open doors—including generational curses—as a legal right to torment. He's very legalistic. He knows the Word better than we do and he uses it. Just like in the garden when the serpent approached Eve to question God's Word. *Did God really say? Did he really mean that?* Test the Word and know God's Word inside and out.

Get in the Word of God and see what it has to say. That's how we resist the enemy. Given half a chance, he'll use the Word against you, but if you know the Word, and stand on it, he's going to flee. There is no good in him; God's goodness repels him.

In the book the Job, we see Satan using the same tactic. He went to God with a proposition. *What about your servant Job? See, he's got this little fear that his kids will never serve you. I bet you if I tempt him, he'll turn on you.* But Job did not fail in temptation; he did not curse God and die as his wife told him to do. The enemy wants to steal our worship and destroy our authority on the earth. He wants to take everything we have—all that Jesus accomplished and gave his life's blood to redeem, including the keys to the kingdom. Satan wants those keys back.

The enemy wants to take us off our mark of bringing forth the kingdom anyway he can. He tries to steal our destiny, purpose, and identity. The younger he can get to us, the more he's going to get us off course. Before long, we begin to think exactly as he wants us to think. He wants us to believe this: *I'm nobody. I'm not loved. God can never love me.* Don't buy the lie.

When we come to a covenant with God though salvation in Jesus Christ, we become heirs with Him. We become co-rulers of his kingdom with Him. We're not stepchildren. He reaches out to each of us and cries with joy: "That's my girl. That's my boy right there. I saw him do this great thing. I saw her do this great thing. They're so full of love and kindness." These are the things that He says about us. The Word says that he dances or delights over us. Yes, he loves us and he cares for us.

Last Call

Our pursuit of spiritual integrity will not end until the day our flesh rests in the grave. Until then, everything we will experience in eternity is affected by what we do here.

> *Once the owner of the house gets up and closes the door, you will*
> *stand outside knocking and pleading, "Sir, open the door for us."*
> *But he will answer, "I don't know you or where you come from."*

Luke 13:25

I can hear this scenario playing out in lives throughout generations.

"Lord, Lord, let me in, let me in!"

"I can't do it," he replies. "I called to you, but you did not respond to me. Do you remember when I called to you and said 'Son or daughter, I love you. Turn to me. Let me heal you. Let me heal that place in you.' And you said 'No, not today. I'm having too much fun. Not today, I kind of like who I am. Not today, Lord, maybe tomorrow. Not today, I'm making too much money. Not today, I don't want to give my money away. Not today, I have people that need me.'"

Everything we are learning here impacts eternity. This is not a self-help course offering seven simple steps to an easy life. We are in the Father's business of redeeming men and women for eternity. The stakes could not be higher.

I remember the Lord calling me into ministry. I reacted by saying: "Lord, you do know I don't love people the way you do, right?"

He replied, "You will."

Sure enough, I am getting there.

> *Here I am! I stand at the door and knock. If anyone hears my voice*
> *and opens the door, I will come in and eat with that person, and*
> *they with me.*

Revelation 3:20

We can only give what we receive. Our work in the kingdom starts with receiving the King and his love. As we grow in his integrity by closing doors that prevent us from experiencing more of his love, we become more like him by sharing truth in love.

3

CHARACTER IDENTITY

Identity defines a person by looks, character and behaviors. It includes the variety of qualities and beliefs that uniquely distinguish them. If a person's character identity is fun and energetic but they walk in sullen and downcast, we would naturally identify an abnormality in that person's behavior. We get to know a person's sense of self and personality over time, and when these are disturbed, we ask: "What has caused a change in that person?"

Life events can cause disturbances in a character identity through emotional trauma or wounded emotions. If a child cries and is harshly scolded and told: "Crying is for babies," that child may grow up hiding their emotions of sadness, loneliness, or loss. The child does not reason that crying is a healthy expression for many different emotions, rather only consider how they feel when getting scolded for crying. Denying such emotions as that child grows to adulthood, a character identity of harshness and rigidity may be acquired. One of the definitions of identity has to do with the continuity of one's personality over time. A single life event can change the course of a person's character identity.

Another form of character identity comes from a condition of behavior based on one's qualities or beliefs that distinguish one person from others. Behavior is an observable action or reaction to internal or external stimuli under given circumstances that helps establish an element of identity. Integrity is a person's adherence to ethical principles and soundness of moral character. From the example above, the grown version of this child has adopted a belief that has altered their sense of integrity. They no longer allow others to see them cry. This characteristic identity through a practice of repetitious behaviors—in this case, not crying—will establish a person's integrity.

For example, somebody who has a lot of father issues may not respond well to a man's authority, advice, or love. They don't trust men. They are more likely to trust a woman. Conversely, someone with mother issues will most likely respond better to a loving papa figure who can bridge that gap and say, "OK, the Father wants to demonstrate his love for you through this father."

In the last chapter, we discussed spiritual integrity and how it related to open doors. When we have open doors, our integrity is readily compromised. We have doors in our past and present that we need to keep shut. There are also doors of the Lord that we need to open and walk through. We need to seize those opportunities as the Lord shows us.

> *May integrity and uprightness protect me, because my hope,*
> *Lord, is in you.*

> Psalm 25:21

Our integrity and uprightness protect us. As long as we walk in our integrity, we will not compromise our walk of righteousness. We are protected. But the moment we compromise, we are likely to make a choice that is other than righteous and holy. Once we create an opening, we're vulnerable.

In the city, you wouldn't leave your front door open because you might not find your home in the same condition you left it. An open door represents an invitation to come in. A closed door provides security and privacy. The same is true with the doors of integrity.

> *Because of my integrity you uphold me and set me in your*
> *presence forever.*

> Psalm 41:12

In the Garden of Eden, Adam and Eve suddenly realized they were naked. But this happened after they lost their spirit glory. Prior to their ignoble fall, the glory of the Lord shined so brightly on them that they only saw the spirit even though they were made of flesh. Their spirit man was their identity, and that is how they identified one another. But the moment they disobeyed God's command, that glory diminished. Through their behavior, their character identity was instantly altered. They looked around and cried: "What is this? Where did the glory go?" They failed to walk in integrity, and they lost God's glory.

When we walk in integrity and righteousness, we are aware that we are seated with Christ. We become full of his glory and are identified by that glory within us. We become one with him—one glory. But if we compromise our integrity, we lose our position with the Father because we've opened a door to vulnerability. We become naked and exposed.

A person's integrity is about behaviors seen and unseen. Will you respond the same way when no one is looking, or when nothing is to be gained? Your personal integrity is connected to how you respond to this question by your behavior. I liken integrity to the two forms of biblical armor: the outer armor in Ephesians 6: 10-18, and the under armor in Exodus 28. We can shine the outer armor, quote scripture, and do good things, but God sees the innermost parts. He sees the heart. He knows every thought. The outer armor is donned so we remember to exercise what is in our heart. The priests of the Old Testament had garments they had to put on before coming before the Lord. The under armor was an important part of that uniform. It was about modesty, concealing the private things. The under armor is how we protect those things that are righteous, pure, and holy. God sees that under armor protects the holy place. The responsibilities of the priests were heavy. If a priest entered God's presence unprepared, he died. This was more than a ritual to the priests; it was protecting that which was holy and vital.

Today, we have mercy because of Jesus. Instead of the Father striking us dead, we get another chance. However, if our under armor is vulnerable—open doors—then we are no longer seated on the mercy seat. That glory diminishes within us, and we become an easy target for the enemy. He comes like a predator circling a wounded bird, basking in our frailty and eager for slaughter.

"Righteousness guards the person of integrity, but wickedness overthrows the sinner."

Proverbs 13:6

Considering this scripture in Proverbs, who is righteousness? Jesus is righteous. He defends us. Just as the priests went to the temple to provide a sacrifice for the people, Jesus, the High Priest, made atonement for us. Jesus' blood symbolically serves as under armor covering our flesh, bringing atonement for our sins. The first demonstration of this comes through salvation in Jesus Christ.

Communion is another symbolic representation of the living sacrifice that Jesus became; we are washing the intimate places of our hearts and minds (flesh) with the cleansing blood of Jesus Christ.

Baptism is a physical expression of the washing away of dirt and sin from our flesh. As an ongoing cleansing, we renew our mind through the washing of the Word over us each day, keeping the flesh clean.

Without these armors of protection, we are opening ourselves to all kinds of spiritual predators. But when we guard our places of integrity and are sealed within Jesus—wearing our armor—nothing can penetrate those defenses. Nothing.

Remove every wicked thing from life, from within and throughout. Choose to be seated in righteousness. Then, when something comes against you, you don't necessarily have to defend yourself. God comes to your defense. He is right here. He will never forsake you.

Be Intentional

We have to put forth the effort to walk in God's integrity. Excellence requires sacrifice; it's part of our redemption. God wants the pure excellent gift. He doesn't want the half-hearted gift. He doesn't want the one that's begrudged. He wants a full, loving gift. So, to keep our spiritual integrity, we must know firstly that God is good.

When we love God, we keep his commandments and love other people. It doesn't matter who we like or dislike. Everyone is entitled to

God's love, and so we give it. Truth is, everyone has redeeming qualities. If you ask the Lord, he'll show you things to like about them. You'll find something to appreciate, especially if you start praying for them. If you start getting to know them better, you will find a connection somewhere. That makes it easier.

Love others. Scripture encourages us to love our neighbors as ourselves.

> *"Honor your father and mother," and "love your neighbor as yourself."*

Matthew 19:19

> *"Love the Lord your God with all your heart and with all your soul and with all your mind and with all your strength.' The second is this: 'Love your neighbor as yourself.' There is no commandment greater than these."*

Mark 12:30-31

Put God and others first. If you want to know how to do that, there are plenty of demonstrations in the Old Testament. Simple things matter. If you borrow somebody's lawnmower, return it with the blade sharpened and gas tank full. If someone brings you a plate of brownies, return the plate with your favorite cookie recipe. In general, care for other people's possessions as you would your own.

When it comes to more serious things—slights, arguments, criticisms, slander or lies, Jesus was unambiguous: Turn the other cheek. The goal is not to gain an upper hand from an exchange, but for others to recognize God's love in you. Winning is not about the last word or the smug walk away. It's about reigning in life as Jesus did. He gave his life for humanity and received a throne at the right hand of God.

Cain's anger with God was so great that it turned into rage, and he violently assaulted his brother. There was no love there. Cain made a judgment in his mind about Abel. *My offering is just as good, even though God said it wasn't.* Cain's sense of righteous indignation against his brother and God fed his rage, and murder was the result.

Judgments are slippery slopes that narrow our identity. When we're openhearted, we become open-minded, and differences that once irritated or repulsed us can become acceptable, even interesting. Our identity grows because we now are so much more accepting of people and their situations.

Does that mean we need to put up with all their stuff? No! We have boundaries for that. But we can love them. We can offer them advice if they ask (but only if they ask). Why cast your pearls before swine? If people don't want to change, they won't, and you can't change them. But if they come to you asking, that's the teachable moment to let Jesus shine through you and give them the Word.

Above all, don't lie, not even to spare their feelings (or your own). You're not doing them any favors; you're trespassing against God. Tell people what they need to hear. Tell them the truth, the whole truth, and trust that the truth shall set them free.

> *Then you will know the truth, and the truth will set you free.*
>
> John 8:32

Remember to couple your truth with mercy. It will win over a harsh judgment every time. As the old expression says: "Honey catches more flies than vinegar." Be sweet. Be kind. Be genuine, however if you're not, people are going to read right through it.

> *For judgment will be merciless to one who has shown no mercy; mercy triumphs over judgment.*
>
> James 2:13 NASB

The last six commandments are these:

> 5. *Honor your father and your mother, so that you may live long in the land the Lord your God is giving you.*
>
> 6. *You shall not murder.*
>
> 7. *You shall not commit adultery.*

8. You shall not steal.

9. You shall not give false testimony against your neighbor.

10. You shall not covet your neighbor's house. You shall not covet your neighbor's wife, or his male or female servant, his ox or donkey, or anything that belongs to your neighbor.

Exodus 20:12-17 (emphasis added)

Commandment five—*honor your father and your mother*—is interesting, oddly placed among murder, adultery, and theft. Obey your parents? One has to wonder if Moses slipped that one in because he was having trouble with his teenagers. And yet we have it echoed in the New Testament by Jesus. Note that the first four commandments are all about his Father God, and then commandment 5 is about his earthly parents, Mary and Joseph, they who stood as surrogates for his heavenly Father.

Joseph was a living example of the Father's love. When Mary became pregnant, he could have put her away, but he didn't. The angel of the Lord informed him of the true nature of Mary's pregnancy and Joseph obeyed, staying with Mary to be an earthly father for Jesus.

What was it like fathering the future savior of the world? Well, being a Jewish family, Joseph likely taught Jesus about the Law. He also taught him a trade—carpentry. And he took him in as his own son. Did he treat him cruelly or unfairly? No. How did we know? By the character of Jesus. He obviously did not have any father issues. Instead, he loved, obeyed, and honored his earthly father as well as his heavenly Father. Jesus was raised well by his earthly parents, caretakers as they were for the eternal Father. This is a role to which all parents must aspire.

Matthew says:

Jesus replied, "And why do you break the command of God for the sake of your tradition? For God said, 'Honor your father and mother' and 'Anyone who curses their father or mother is to be put to death.' But you say that if anyone declares that what might

have been used to help their father or mother is 'devoted to God,'
they are not to 'honor their father or mother' with it. Thus, you
nullify the Word of God for the sake of your tradition.

Matthew 15:3-6

Here's my cultural paraphrase of what Jesus was saying in this scripture:

Don't talk badly about your parents. Don't even denounce them, by saying "I
wish I'd never known you. I wish you weren't my parents." Don't do that, because
they raised you. They invested time and money into you. They loved you. They
nurtured you. They had compassion on you when you should've probably had your
bottom whooped.

Further, don't give to God what is owed to your parents. If you owe your
parents money, don't say: "I gave that as an offering, and I can't pay you. I don't
have it, Mom. I gave it to God. Whoa! You should bless me because I bless God."
No! God says to honor that obligation. Honor your word to them. Honor your
parents because they probably need it. They definitely would need it more than God
because God doesn't need it. Pay them what you owe. Don't leave a debt to your
parents. If you have any unpaid debts to your parents, pay them. You owe them!

God gave us these ten rules of measure because we often think: "I'm a good person." Well, are we? Do we remember the Sabbath day and keep it holy? Do we take a day of rest? Even if it can't be on the Sabbath—Saturday, Sunday or whatever you observe—do we take a day of rest to honor the Lord? Yes, rest honors God as much as it honors us. After all, Jesus said:

Then he [Jesus] said to them, "The Sabbath was made for man,
not man for the Sabbath.

Mark 2:27

Peacekeepers and Peacemakers

Conflict revolves around peacekeeping and peacemaking. These two words are often used interchangeably, and yet scripturally, they are different. A peacekeeper seeks to preserve the status quo. A peacemaker promotes what is right and holy.

For example, in my country, the United States, we are currently in a state of peace; we are not actively at war. Yes, there are rumors of war, but no actual war. We do have forces stationed around the world that are engaged in minor conflicts, but overall, we are in a time of peace.

Peacekeepers maintain that state of peace. It doesn't matter who is in government. It doesn't matter who's saying what or the issues under consideration. A peacekeeper's goal is simply to keep the peace. While national leaders have personal viewpoints or preferences, peacekeepers work to maintain whatever state of peace is in existence. Even when there is an evil ruler, peacekeepers will do whatever is necessary to appease that ruler. They are not judging good or evil; rather, they are maintaining and defending the ruler's definition of peace.

Conversely, peacemakers stand ready to engage for what is morally right. They do whatever is required to move things into a state of righteousness and holiness. We, as Christ-ones, contend in this way through spiritual battle. It's how we choose to do the right thing. The way of the peacemaker is difficult. A peacemaker suffers conflict to establish a state of righteousness against popularity. It takes discipline to maintain integrity. It takes willpower and strength.

The enemy will use distractions to get us off course from the primary objective. These distractions are typically associated with personal drama through the use of others. To establish God's kingdom on earth, we must be focused and not allow the drama to take us off the peacemaking path.

Choosing Our Battles

When faced with conflict, we must choose our battles wisely. There are some battles we are meant to fight and others we are meant to avoid. When we confront spiritual warfare, we better know if it's our battle or not. When we engage in battles not intended for us, we get hurt.

Part of choosing our battles is knowing that each is fought differently. Like the various branches of our military, some battles are fought in the air, some on land, and others on the sea. Sometimes it is a prolonged engagement. Other times it is a quick hit and get out—special forces style.

Sometimes we're called to assignments to be fought privately. Other times, God tells us to assemble a team to fight together.

Recently, a friend was doing spiritual warfare alone, but it was meant for a team. He struggled until he realized it was not a one-person endeavor. "I get it now," he told me. "I was not supposed to go into that warfare by myself, but I did. And I left myself completely exposed." I replied, "It happens more than you think."

We have to know the assignment and the vision of the Lord for a battle. We have to know whether we're meant to go in as a single covert agent or with a team. Do we need the whole regiment on the battlefield with us, facing the enemy in a frontal assault? The Lord will show us what kind of warfare we're in.

We also need to know who our enemy is. Are we fighting an individual or a spirit? Most of the time, it's a spirit that looks like an individual or group of individuals. We need to know who the enemy really is.

Resist the Enemy

After teaching us to pray based on the key elements of the Ten Commandments, Jesus continued preparing us to resist the enemy and serve God.

No one can serve two masters. Either you will hate the one and love the other, or you will be devoted to the one and despise the other. You cannot serve both God and money.

Matthew 6:24

No man can serve two masters. We can't appease the devil and please God. We've got to be sure in our way. There is a narrow path, and we must stay on it. We cannot stumble and expect to stay well. Certainly, we do stumble at times, and God has mercy for that, but it opens doors for us that we must close.

When we fail to resist the enemy, we compromise our spiritual integrity. Therefore, anything that we do not deal with in the spirit realm regarding open doors can be passed on through our generational line.

Generational curses exist. As such, we can't serve two masters. We can't walk in our identity as Christ-ones and also respond to curses embedded in our generational line.

We can see examples in comparing contrasts between Jesus and Cain. Cain gave in to his flesh and was cursed. Everywhere he went, he was tormented. He worried that somebody would come back and kill him because of what he had done. In response to Cain's plea, God marked his face. Henceforth, Cain was known throughout the land, but he continued to live in fear. He was tormented the rest of his life because he did not go back and ask God to forgive him. Had he called upon the name of the Lord for forgiveness, God would have answered him just as he did about the mark on his forehead.

Touching God's Heart

A man named Cornelius appears in Acts 10. Cornelius was not Jewish, he was Italian. And yet he respects the land, follows the laws, and does what was right. He is good to others: the poor, widows, and orphans, and he prays regularly to God.

Growing within Cornelius is a yearning: *God, I want to experience what people are talking about, and I hear it's for the Jews.*

In response, the angel of the Lord comes to Cornelius with good news. Because of his love for others, the Lord heard his prayers and honored the desire of his heart. *Cornelius, I'm going to send a couple of guys over here. They're going to bring Peter back and then things are going to happen.* The next thing you know, Cornelius' servants set out to track down Peter.

Meanwhile, Peter is hungry. He goes to the rooftop, and he prays. The Lord gives him a vision and starts sending him food through this vision. An open heaven is happening, and things come through the spirit realm. But Peter resists: *God, I can't eat that. I have not defiled my body. I can't eat that.*

The Lord persists, however: *I am sending it to you to eat, and you're telling me that it's not good enough for you? I made it. What the Law has said is unclean, I'm saying it is now clean and you can partake of it because I have sent it*

Peter resists a second time, but the Lord emphasizes again: *I've blessed it, I've made it clean.* Soon, the servants of Cornelius arrive with an intriguing proposition: *Our master just had a vision of an angel of the Lord. He sent us to you. Are you Peter?* And Peter's excited because he's beginning to connect the dots: *I just had this vision of God telling me to eat his stuff that I've never tasted in my life.*

Peter recognizes God's voice: *You're going to go to this man. He's not a Jew but I'm sending you to him because I love him and I've called him clean. I've called him and said he's worthy. He is worthy of my Son's blood.*

Peter then follows the servants back to Cornelius' house. Cornelius gets saved — his whole family and his servants, also. Revival breaks out in the land. God moves mightily during Peter's visit there in the land. Because Cornelius loved others and it touched God's heart, the Holy Spirit was poured out upon the Gentiles.

Let this story challenge you. What have you done recently to touch God's heart? What would it take to do something extra to convey appreciation or love?

4

IDENTIFYING CONFLICT

God created us to have a free will. He did not create us to control us, but we were created out of his love for us. Since sin entered into creation and caused a separation from God, creation experiences conflict. Conflict means: "To come into collision or disagreement; to be contradictory." We can activate conflict simply by being contradictory. We don't have to intend outright confrontation, but we all have opinions—what we consider good or bad, what we like and don't like. These variables create measures of conflict.

How Conflict Affects Our Bodies

We experience conflict within and without. Day and night, we are in personal conflict of some sort. Our body's immune system is in constant conflict whether we are aware of it or not. Its purpose is to recognize biological conflict and respond appropriately. The Lord taught our bodies how to deal with certain forms of conflict when He created us.

In addition to bodily conflicts, we struggle daily in personal conflicts between soul and spirit. We deal with these conflicts in many ways---some that are healthy, bringing about a constructive resolution, and others that are unhealthy.

The healthy objective of conflict is to find a satisfactory resolution. Ignoring an issue does not cause it to go away. Instead, it festers and eventually develops into something destructive.

There is a temptation to hide personal issues, making them invisible and muted. But we know what those stuffed-away issues eventually do: Boom! They *will* come out in some form. One possible manifestation is some type of infirmity or disease. Unaddressed conflict opens the doors to a host of maladies.

Our bodies are designed to constantly deal with the effects of conflict. Yet, if it is not resolved, our physical health can begin to reflect our inward sickness: ulcers, high blood pressure, aches and pains.

Stress is meant to be worked out and processed through the body. We're not supposed to hold it inwardly; we are meant to express it. There are healthy forms of expressing stress, and there are unhealthy forms. As long as we merely cope or avoid conflict by stuffing it within us—unresolved conflict—we're creating an unhealthy internal imbalance.

The healthy way to deal with stress is to come before the Father and say, "Lord, I'm in conflict. I need a healthy balance." In response, Holy Spirit will begin to talk with us. He will be our teacher, leading us to a healthy resolution. He will talk to us about strategies, how to approach the situation, illuminate our own perspectives, and open our hearts, as necessary.

Recently, a young woman was undergoing deep, personal examination with Holy Spirit of conflicts in her life, especially with God. All of a sudden, she said, "I'm angry with God. He didn't answer prayer and I'm angry."

She was experiencing the conflict that she had been avoiding. It was there and it was real, but to address it meant that she was going to have to take corrective action. We may be able to brush off other interpersonal conflicts, but when it comes to grievances with God, that's where the rubber meets the road.

Before we can go deeper in God—before we can experience a deeper love in Him and fully trust Him and put all of our loyalty in Him—we have to resolve certain conflicts. We must learn to let go of those things and say, "You know what? I don't understand it, and I may not ever understand it, but I know that I know that you, Lord, are sufficient to complete it."

I understand the difficulty. Sometimes I get angry when God doesn't answer prayer. But I have learned to sit back and say, "Lord, in your time.

It may not be the appointed time for now. It may not be what I think it should be. You are all-knowing, and I am not. My knowing is limited, and any knowledge that I do gain is through the anointing and power of your Holy Spirit. So I leave it with you, and I trust that you have this."

Forms of Conflict

Conflict also appears in controversy, discord of action or antagonism. Conflict appears in any type of opposition, such as the interests of principles. The very fact that our country has two primary and opposing political parties creates conflict. Those parties were purposefully created to oppose one another, established in the hope of bringing balance of power and influence.

Conflict appears where there is incompatibility of ideas, desires, events, or activities. Essentially, conflict is a part of living. It appears in marriage, parenting, friendships, even in solitude. If you lived alone on a desert island, you'd still be contending for your life; it'd be you against the elements. You have to start a fire, find food and water, build shelter, and send smoke signals to get rescued. No matter where we live, conflict is a part of existence.

Of course, conflict is not necessarily negative. It can be beneficial. It's the healthy tension that keeps people engaged, respectfully debating, sharpening their understanding and challenging assumptions. This allows us the benefit of exercising the commands God established in Genesis to multiply (seed), subdue the earth (land) and rule over the living creatures (livelihood), commands reinforced later by the covenant with Moses.

Patterns of Conflict

There are three negative patterns of behavior that are often found in conflict that must be avoided to maintain a healthy identity. They are often referred to as a drama triangle and include the persecutor, the rescuer, and the victim. The Drama Triangle is where the ships of our relationships are capsized in the sea of drama. Due to the nature of the triangle, the victim sits atop as all focus is on them. The predator and rescuer sit on either side. The direction of behaviors flows on any side of the triangle to another.

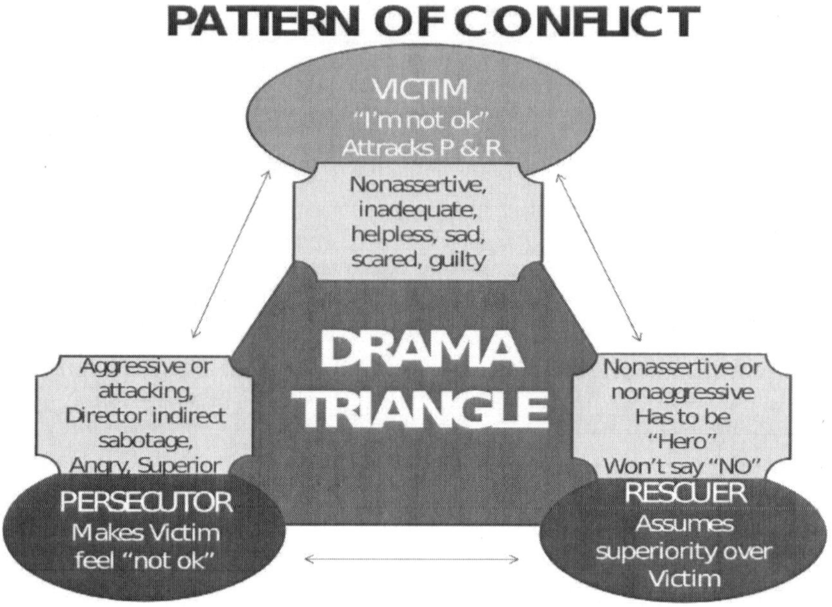

PATTERN OF CONFLICT

VICTIM
"I'm not ok"
Attracks P & R

Nonassertive,
inadequate,
helpless, sad,
scared, guilty

DRAMA TRIANGLE

Aggressive or
attacking,
Director indirect
sabotage,
Angry, Superior

PERSECUTOR
Makes Victim
feel "not ok"

Nonassertive or
nonaggressive
Has to be
"Hero"
Won't say "NO"

RESCUER
Assumes
superiority over
Victim

FIGURE 2 – Drama Triangle Diagram

A victim will sometimes assume false responsibility for something. For instance, if a marriage has spousal abuse, the victim may say they did something which set off or caused the abuse. Some victims will accept an identity of victim by agreeing "I'm not OK." This draws the rescuer and predator to a victim like a shark to fish blood. Behaviors of a victim include but are not limited to feelings of non-assertiveness, inadequacy, helplessness, sadness, fear, and guilt. If a victim fails to thrive in recovery, they set themselves up for perpetuating victimization. For instance, a child whose victimization is not realized to allow them to receive necessary healing will be victimized again and again. Individuals who are under a 'spirit of Victim' or 'victim mentality' will actually thrive on the attention that being 'victimized' affords them. When this is the case, the victim will pine and whine as they are the focus of all victimization to seek out any or all attention. The victimization may have occurred, but they get stuck in an unhealthy attraction for attention and may recreate false encounters of victimization.

The predator will abuse the victim verbally or physically. The predator reinforces to the victim that they are 'not OK'. The predator will use the rescuer. A predator is aggressive or attacking. They are the director of direct or indirect sabotage. They have deep-rooted anger with a superiority complex. They feel justified to act badly because the rescuer witnesses it but doesn't speak up. The predator will blame the victim for their behavior.

The rescuer is also non-assertive or nonaggressive. The rescuer plays the hero to the victim and pretends to be on their side while allowing the predator to get away with bad behavior. The rescuer will not say, 'no'. The rescuer assumes superiority over the victim and sometimes joins the predator in the emotional abuse of the victim.

The rescuer or predator could have been a victim at some point. All of these components of the Drama Triangle are interchangeable. In a weakened or careless moment, anyone could fall into one or more of these categories. But when we see it, we know there are some deep wounds—things that they've not resolved, maybe years or decades old, layers upon layers of conflict where emotional wounds occurred. They obviously need inner healing from unhealthy behaviors.

So, when you observe someone behaving like a victim, it's a cue to be hands-off. They're choosing a behavior. You can't talk to them because they can't hear you. No matter how carefully you correct them, all they will hear is a persecutor's voice speaking accusations to them, telling them what they got wrong.

Both persecutor and rescuer run to the victim. The persecutor likes reminding the victim of their failures and accusing them of their weaknesses. The rescuer arrives to save the day, commiserating with the victim and fixing their problems. But guess what? The victim has to walk out their situation. They have to find their path. And let me tell you, you can give them all the advice in the world, but you can't make them change. The truth of the matter is this: They may not *want* to change. And if the victim doesn't want to change, no one can help them.

When we feel the urgent need to rescue, we can put ourselves above God, feeling confident that we understand what is happening and can fix it. But remember: Stay in your lane. It's not your job to fix anyone, and it's not their job to fix you. They need to stay in their lane, you need to stay in your lane. Love each other and let's all stay in our respective lanes. I can reach across your lane and hold your hand, and when you're struggling, I can hold you. I can help ensure you don't wear out or go over the edge or end up in a ditch. But we have to allow each person to walk their own path. The Word says: *"Work out your salvation with fear and trembling"* (Philippians 2:12).

Why is that? Because there's conflict. It's not our job to fix other people. It's our job to direct them to God, the true Fixer Upper.

I'll never forget the day the Lord said to me, "I gave you babies for a season. And that season is over."

He wasn't telling me I had fulfilled my responsibility to raise them. He was revealing to me that I was becoming a stumbling block in the ways I was trying to interact with them, standing between them and himself. When I got out of the way and stopped trying to rescue my adult children, the Lord properly aligned my position with my children. Now, I only offer advice when it is asked of me. This advice will direct them back to hear what the Lord says.

Communication is key when you're dealing with conflict. We have to acknowledge and communicate the boundaries we've established. For instance, a rescuer has a hard time saying "no." In fact, they don't say "no" to anything. They want to be a peacekeeper, not a peacemaker. They want to make everybody happy. They're agreeable. They go along with the flow. They want it all fixed. They're the rescuer. They'll patch things over, believing they've resolved a problem when really, they've "fixed" a gaping hole by sticking their finger in it—a hole that starts bleeding again the moment they leave.

We learn when it's appropriate to say "no." We also learn when it's appropriate to say, "You know what? I think I'd like to try that. Let's give it a season. Let's test this if we're not sure. Let's see what the Father says." Boundaries allow us to explore healthfully.

Rules and boundaries are established for good reason. They protect us from foolish vulnerabilities. It's important to regularly reexamine these boundaries and reestablish them. The people who consider themselves close to you: Are they respecting your boundaries?

A child was given a firm boundary: "You can go spend time in *this* place, but under no circumstances, are you to go to *that* place." No means no. And yet, when the child was with {?}, the child ended up at *that* place.

Was that honoring boundaries? Of course not. Breaking an individual's boundaries does not show honor to the boundaries or to that relationship. When your boundaries are not honored, it is up to you to restate the boundary, answer any questions about that boundary, and have the person restate the boundary. If the boundary is still not respected, it is time to withdraw the possibility of dishonoring that boundary. It's up to us to reinforce our boundaries while, at the same time, respecting the boundaries of others.

Avoiding Drama

Learn to discern when it is appropriate to be a peacekeeper or a peacemaker. To avoid drama, it is usually best to be the peacekeeper; walk away, keep your integrity, hold your tongue, and ask: "Is this worthy of my engagement?"

There are conflicts that we might wish to avoid but have to confront, saying: "Look, this conflict is not healthy for me, and it's not healthy for you. We need to change a pattern here." Ask what the Word says about this and draw Jesus' wisdom into your response. This is the time to be the peacemaker. There are some things we have to engage.

When I am seriously struggling with something—when I am in a painful and dangerous state—I cocoon for a while. It's not meant to last for weeks or months, but only for about three days. I do this for two reasons:

1. To hear what the Lord is saying on the matter.

Find out what God is saying through his Word and through prayer. Perhaps ask: "Father, what do you say about this matter? Is this something I need to confront? How do you want me to handle this? Or do I even need to handle it at all? Is this something you're dealing with?" Make sure this situation doesn't take root.

2. Avoid my personal pain inflicting pain on others.

If an animal gets hit by a car and you go over and pick up it up, it's going to bite. Why? Because it's hurting. It's a natural protective reaction to react to others in a negative way when they are trying to help.

Cocooning allows time to withdraw until the pain eases up and resolution comes without inflicting residual pain to others around us. Stand in faith. Call two trusted prayer partners when the conflict is intense. We're not meant to fight all battles alone, right? That's why we have one another.

Be careful about cocooning, however, because it can become a pattern of avoidance. Instead, set a finite period of seclusion to make sure that you walk out that trial well. Let one or two people know you are entering a cocoon, so they can check on you to ensure it doesn't turn into something counterproductive.

During the cocooning process, ask what is causing this reaction. "Why is this issue bothering me? What's going on? Have I opened a door? Is there a door open in my generational line?"

Everyone overreacts from time to time—situations that don't merit the reaction they receive. A simple conversation can lead to an outburst. What just happened? Something triggered an emotion that caused the out-of-proportion reaction. We need to identify the triggers behind the outburst.

Conflict is often a part of growth. As people delve deeper into the glory of God, it pulls deep-rooting thoughts and attitudes to the surface to be exposed and dealt with. People find themselves saying: "Where on earth did that come from?" Remember, God is renewing his glory in us, and deep healing happens in that place of deep glory.

Here is a wise standard concerning conflict: Don't let the issue go unaddressed for so long that it festers and settles deep within you. The Word says,

> *"In your anger do not sin": Do not let the sun go down while you are still angry and do not give the devil a foothold.*

> Ephesians 4:26-27

Be wise. Deal with conflict as soon as you can; you're not promised tomorrow. Do you want to win? What if you're overcome in your sleep? What if the enemy builds things into your dreams? We've got to be accountable for our part in a conflict and not let issues go without resolution.

Offense is a choice, but if someone offends you, go talk with them. To tell someone else is creating more discord by compromising your integrity. Your words are important. Give them life to bring healing to the conflict rather than sowing seeds of destruction through relationships. If you mischaracterize someone to another, you damage their character identity. Even if you reconcile, your words have already darkened the reputation of their integrity through your inability to process conflict. A person can be as offensive to you as they choose to be—that is their choice. But for you to *take* offense—to be offended—that is *your* choice.

Dealing with Conflict

When faced with conflict, we must decide how to deal with it. The book of Proverbs gives us several indicators by which to identify the sources of conflict.

> *Who plots evil with deceit in his heart—he always stirs up conflict.*

> Proverbs 6:14

> *Hatred stirs up conflict, but love covers over all wrongs.*

Proverbs 10:12

A hot-tempered person stirs up conflict, but the one who is patient calms a quarrel.

Proverbs 15:18

A perverse person stirs up conflict, and a gossip separates close friends.

Proverbs 16:28

An angry person stirs up conflict, and a hot-tempered person commits many sins.

Proverbs 29:22

As I think, so I am. My body follows my mind. If my body sends a signal that says: "Breathe," guess what? I'm going to breathe. It is hardwired in my physiology. I don't even have to be conscious. From our mindsets come our behaviors—the manner in which we act. Our behaviors are observable activities that manifest in the physical part of our beings.

This is where our outer armor is so important. It is used to ensure that we behave righteously in any conflict so that our spiritual integrity or under armor remains intact. Since our actions speak louder than words, it is important that our words align with the integrity of holy under armor and our actions as peacemakers are out of love. This will protect us from every accusation of the enemy. The Word is truly clear on how to deal with conflict whether it is with oneself, another, or the enemy of God. We are to follow what Jesus taught and demonstrated in his Word.

The conflict may come from something internal or external, but our behaviors that conflict with other people will manifest in the physical. Even the choice to take a passive position will affect our behavior, such as walking away from a situation.

What causes fights and quarrels among you? Don't they come from your desires that battle within you?

James 4:1

James is telling us that we have battles because we have an open door somewhere and that's the thing that's raging. This is what happened to Cain—Abel's brother—in Genesis. He had an open door of jealousy and rage stirring things up and it eventually manifested in the physical as the act of murdering his brother.

> *For the flesh desires what is contrary to the Spirit, and the Spirit*
> *what is contrary to the flesh. They are in conflict with each other,*
> *so that you are not to do whatever you want.*

Galatians 5:17

We can't live out all of our fleshly impulses and expect to live holy lives. The flesh—that part of us that wants to be disobedient—is destructive. It leads to death.

> *For the wages of sin is death, but the gift of God is eternal life in*
> *Christ Jesus our Lord.*

Romans 6:23

When dealing with wounded people, it has been proven time and again that they will wound other people. Below, I am going to list characteristics of destructive behaviors that can occur. Please take note and evaluate any patterns of these behaviors within yourself or others. I urge you to incorporate healthy boundaries and tools to help move you away from destructive behaviors. If a situation becomes violent, CALL 911.

Look for these traits when determining if there is a conflict:

Conflict Behaviors

- Fails to follow rules or to cooperate with others
- Says one thing then does another, changes mind from what's been agreed upon, or often commits to something only to cancel at last minute
- Identifies as a victim
- Creates negativity, gossip, rumors toward others or positions others on 'sides'

- When they are confronted, cries, yells, shows anger, insults, or mocks the other
- May use family or 'I feel Like God said' as excuses to cause division or pull others from the group

Nuisance Behaviors

- Gets defensive when criticized; or goes into denial
- Uses sarcasm when confronted
- Makes excuses to divert or get the focus off important issues
- Negative and complains yet unwilling to change
- Blames others; doesn't take personal responsibility

Violent Behaviors

- There is a history of being bullied or a victim
- Shows little regard for the property of others' and/or animals
- Typically, does not allow others to see them in a weakened state; vulnerable or crying
- Threatens physical force or intention of harm
- Physical force that may result or intention to intimidate, cause injury, damage, or death
- Weapons, attacks, displays physical actions mentioned above

Tips to Live By

- Ask yourself if the conflict really matters; you may not like the end result
- Being right may not resolve the conflict; giving grace isn't losing power
- Know when the conflict is ensuing and act with discernment
- Use open-ended questions to bring clarity to the situation
- You can't fix people, but you can speak the truth in love
- Conflict is stressful
- Don't get sucked into the drama
- It's not always about you / Sometimes it is really all about you

5

CONFLICT RESOLUTION

Conflict resolution means something different to everyone. Peacekeepers don't care about the condition or circumstances they are in. They only seek to preserve the status quo. They just want to keep everybody happy. But peacemakers see what needs to be accomplished and are willing to engage—even to provoke conflict—to establish or restore a healthy environment.

It is wrong to conclude that a person is not a peacemaker simply because they are constantly stirring up issues. Rather, that person understands how things should be for the greatest, long-term peace. They'll say, "OK, this is how we have to do this because we're headed in a wrong direction. We need to correct; otherwise we're all going to fall off the cliff." Because they see impending disaster, they put themselves at the forefront and prevent it from happening.

If a child plays in the road, a peacemaker will take initiative to redirect the child from potential danger. A peacemaker works from the offensive. However, a peacekeeper also works from the defensive. A peacekeeper will allow the child to keep playing in the road, placing the responsibility to identify danger on the child and any oncoming traffic, but he will spring into action if the child is in immediate danger.

Pattern of Resolution

The Pattern of Resolution is a triangle of healthy communication practices used in the midst of conflict. The pattern of Resolution has one point at the bottom called Vulnerable. One of the top corners is called Assertive and the other top corner is Caring.

Be vulnerable to:

- State how the conflict affected you emotionally, physically, or spiritually
- Discover what part you played in the conflict
- State your expected outcome

Be assertive to:

- Confront the issue that causes conflict with the individual(s)
- State the undesired behavior
- Take ownership of your part in the conflict
- Apologize and ask for forgiveness for your part

Be caring to:

- Validate their feelings
- Listen effectively

PATTERN OF RESOLUTION

FIGURE 3 – Pattern of Resolution Diagram

Healthy resolution to conflict requires vulnerability. Be open. "Hey, I'm just struggling with something. I know you didn't mean it. I know because of your character. But this is how, at that time, I took what you said/did. So maybe you can help me understand what was going on around me that could have triggered this emotion in me."

They might respond with: "You know what? I was frustrated at the time, and you probably felt it. I apologize."

When we expose our vulnerability—our under-armor garment—we enter an intimate place of humility. God uses a humble heart. He moves through humility. In contrast, if we go in proud and hot-tempered, our situation is not going to be truly resolved. It will most likely get worse.

Now, humble does not mean passive. We can be humble and assertive at the same time. Assertiveness says, "I have needs. If this relationship is going to work, let me communicate to you these boundaries." For example: "I don't feel comforted by your underhanded criticism. That is not healthy for me. When you tease me, not recognizing what you're doing, it hurts me. Please stop."

If the other person doesn't adjust as you've asked them to, uphold your boundary. "You know what? I have discovered that this is an unhealthy relationship. And because of that, I'm going to start cutting back my time with you. I love you, but I don't deserve this. I love myself enough that I'm not going to allow you to talk to me that way. I don't dishonor you and I would appreciate that you would return the same."

As hearts are expressed and thoughts are conveyed, show you care by really listening to the other person. Listening is a fruit of honor but does not make room for drama. When you honor someone, you give them time and room to freely express themselves in a calm and non-accusatory manner. When the conversation turns emotional in a dishonoring way, it is time to politely leave the discussion until both parties can resume with honor.

Within this triangle of resolution, are three necessary constants: communicate their feeling and desired outcome, validate feelings and communication through effective listening practices, and breathe before responding. Avoid allowing the resolution process to become volatile or out of control. The last thing you will want to do is inflate the situation or allow other offenses to occur. Communicate from all aspects of the triangle of resolution.

Establish the Expectation

Recently, I spoke with a pastor about a situation he was facing. For a period of time, a person would flow in and out of their church community. The time came when responsibilities were assigned within the church. He was not given a task and took offense to being overlooked. Unfortunately, instead of addressing the issue, he acted in classic avoidance mode, going around to different people in their church, stirring up discord over his being overlooked for a post, regardless of the fact that he had only attended a service twice in the past year.

In speaking with the pastor, I asked, "Remind me again what your reasons were for not giving this person a position?" The pastor explained where this individual had fallen short in their commitment to the body. These shortcomings weighed heavily when considering them for a position. His said items such as regular attendance, faithful tithing, and occasional volunteering, were important. I asked, "Do you have these qualities in writing anywhere?" He said, "Well, no."

I encouraged him to write down the standards by which he considered people for duties, and to adopt that list into the bylaws of his church so that these expectations were clearly communicated. The bottom line is that expectations can't be met unless they are communicated.

Clearly communicating the expectations of any vision or relationship is a vital tool, just as giving a job description when you hire someone.

Below are signs of a caring listener.

1. Maintain Eye Contact.

Nothing says "I'm paying attention" like looking someone in the eye. The eyes are the portal to the soul. Words are important, but meaningful contact is made on a deeper level. You can't make meaningful contact while glancing at your phone or the clock or a computer screen. It takes conscious effort.

2. Appropriate Responses

Offer an appropriate response to what's being said. How many times do we catch ourselves giving an absent-minded response that's not invested and accurate? Perhaps we are on the phone with a friend, and she says, "My neighbor just died." Your response is, "That's cool."

Wait, what?

It's easy to drift away from full attention in a phone conversation because there's no eye contact. However, take or make the call, be fully invested in the conversation. Learn to respond in a consistent manner so the people around you learn to trust you and your consistent character. Of course, you won't interact with each person identically, but the mature listener should demonstrate a stable, consistent approach—much like a mother who speaks similarly to each of her children but deals with their challenges differently, depending on the child.

3. Encourage

When dealing with people's conflicts, it is important to not rush them along. Give them room to fully make their points. If they walk away feeling that they've not been heard and were unable to unburden themselves, they're still going to have the issue on their minds and hearts. Let them express themselves. It doesn't matter what they're saying, it doesn't matter how vulgar or how bad it is. It matters that they feel listened to. Engage and be receptive to them.

"I hear that you think this of <so and so>."

"I apologize if you felt that I committed this oversight."

"I apologize if in any way you felt this way."

You may be entirely right in the matter but rather than stating your case, however, generously choose to allow them to speak their piece. You don't want to be the stumbling block that's keeping them bottled up.

4. Speak Sparingly

Keep conflict resolution on point, redirecting if necessary. It's OK to say, "OK, I realize we're getting off track a little bit, but can we go back to this because I want to make sure we're fully resolved in this area before we move on." Make sure the matter is resolved. Make sure there is nothing unaddressed. To close the discussion, ask open-ended questions.

"How did that make you feel?"

"What happened next?"

"What could I do better?"

5. Validate

"I hear what you are saying."

"I can see how you may have come to that conclusion."

"I understand how you feel."

Even if a person's feelings are misguided, they are real. Feelings constitute reality and vary from person to person. Most likely, they will clash with your feelings. Expect it and set aside your feelings to allow the other person to express themselves.

For instance, my husband and I have four children. They all grew up in the same home with the same parents and lived in the same places. But their life experiences are different. With this in mind, you have to be open to the experience of another. Appreciate their perspective. It may not be anywhere near what you perceived, but you need to allow them to communicate their side. Validate that they saw things differently.

"Now I understand where the miscommunication was. What can I do to help?"

6. Email is Limited

Do not use email to attempt resolution. Can you fully convey your feelings in an email? No, you cannot. There is no vocal inflection in email. It doesn't matter how well we write. The recipient of that email is not where you are, mentally or emotionally. They may not receive it with the same spirit in which it was written. It's not contingent upon how we write it but upon the mood they are in when they read it.

I've had my own business for years. I get emails from all kinds of people in all kinds of places. If an email hits me wrong, I get up and walk away. I typically go outside and make a clean break of that topic in my mind. I won't even look at the email again until I have a fresh perspective. When I'm ready, I read the email again before I respond. Many times, in rereading the email, I realize it doesn't say what I thought it said and I understand more clearly what the writer was communicating.

For that reason, I have learned to check my emotional state before I write an email. I do this through prayer. It's email and therefore is limited. It only takes a simple mistake for a situation to boil over, evoking an unintended response on the other end, and leaving the sender wondering, "What just happened?"

Simple misunderstandings happen in so many areas of our lives. In the workplace, an email can be the flashpoint that divides departments. Among friends, one might accuse another, saying, "You sent a hateful email." Was it really hateful, or were they just stating the fact? Perhaps they needed a resolution; Are you the person or group they needed to bring that problem to? If not, then who?

The key to resolving email issues, then, is to not take email personally, although email is not the method to use when resolving conflict. It is alright to summarize the outcome of the resolution by identifying the issue, list any new behaviors or boundaries being implemented and state the overall outcome or progress of the discussion.

7. Closure

Validate, empathize, apologize, and take responsibility for your part. Then bring closure to the matter. If, however, that person comes back to you a week later and starts accusing you all over again, the terms have changed. You can say: "Oh, oh. Wait. We dealt with this. Remember? We sat down and talked about this. Remember? And I apologized to you for this? Now, have I done something new since then?"

If they keep bringing that up, there's a greater problem. Something's off somewhere. Try to get to the root issue, because whatever they originally addressed with you wasn't the core matter. There's something much deeper that needs to be addressed.

Personal Conflict

Have you ever experienced that ugly twinge when a certain person's name comes into your thoughts? That inner pang tells you that you've got some internal work to do.

Personally, conflict is usually unexpected, and I am often surprised out of my oblivion. When I get an unexpected call, I usually have to take a moment to get an intentional perspective. If I don't, the conflict starts to fester within me. By stepping back, I can return and say, "OK, now that my flesh had been flushed, let's think objectively. I can start addressing the situation with my spirit man, asking: "What does God say?"

Sometimes it takes a minute to make that mental switch between our flesh and the Spirit. That's OK. Maturity knows that distinction and pauses to make the shift. As we work to prevent unnecessary, destructive eruption, it is OK at times to walk away, cool off and come back.

I'm a deeply passionate individual, and in my younger years I was quite volatile. When I am involved in something, I am entirely invested. Even in my facial expressions, hand gestures and body language— everything of me is saying, "I believe in this. I am fully vested. I'm going for it."

I am that way with everything I do. So when I experience a passionate conflict, I need a moment to ask, "Why am I feeling this way? What's going on? Can I just sulk for a minute? Can I be a child for two seconds, sticking out my lower lip?" I truly have these conversations with God, but not as often as I used to.

Personal Story

One time I was working out my passionate reaction to a conflict in the healthiest way I knew. I was furious because somebody had just publicly shredded one of my children's prophetic giftings. It was quite an ordeal.

The Lord said to me, "It's OK. I'm going to give you an assignment. You're going to pray for the person who criticized your child." I responded, "Oh no, I'm praying right now that you just take them away or I'll help them move away!"

I'm being real. You don't mess with a mama and her babies.

But I kept talking with the Lord. Eventually, I said, "I know I've got to do the right thing. I know it. But can you just let me have my tantrum?"

He said, "Yes. I can let you have your tantrum...because I know that when you're done, you're going to turn around and crawl right into my lap. Then I'm going to hold you, and when you get down, you're going to do the right thing."

I was awed. God blessed me in spite my tantrums. His words were cutting to me because I knew he was loving me in spite of my temper, even though what he really desired was for me not to have a tantrum at all.

This began in me a work of love and humility to resolves those tantrums and forgiveness toward the one who had offended me and my son. Do tantrums still want to come up? Oh yes, they do, but God is still working. When those outbursts flare, he simply says, "When you're ready, come talk to me. We'll work it out." Through his patient, deep love, my tantrums don't happen nearly as often as they once did. Over the years, I've learned how to walk in forgiveness efficiently and effectively without offense.

Forgiveness makes our hearts get lighter when we forgive. That sense of dread or anger deep in the gut leaves when we can forgive someone. We need to forgive and move on. "You know what, I apologized, and I forgave you. I am sorry that we even had this misunderstanding. I let it go. I just want you to know I love you."

> *If your brother or sister sins, go and point out their fault, just between the two of you. If they listen to you, you have won them over. But if they will not listen, take one or two others along, so that 'every matter may be established by the testimony of two or three witnesses.' If they still refuse to listen, tell it to the church; and if they refuse to listen even to the church, treat them as you would a pagan or a tax collector.*

Matthew 18:15-17

Bringing others to conflict closure exposes the spirit of the disagreement. Often, the spiritual root must be dealt with in prayer before we can move on. In all things, remember that you represent Christ to them.

> *In everything set them an example by doing what is good. In your teaching show integrity, seriousness and soundness of speech that cannot be condemned, so that those who oppose you may be ashamed because they have nothing bad to say about us.*

Titus 2:7-8

How we deal with conflict in these situations will give evidence to how healthy our under armor is. If it is spotless and pure, we will be able to deal patiently and thoroughly with others in their complaints. Be consistent to show righteousness.

Mistakes happen, but they should not continue happening. Once you forgive and forget, let go and move on. If you don't let go, it will be hard to heal. That inner barb will be a constant reminder in your soul. You've got to let go. It doesn't matter who was right. Forgive them and pray for them. Don't bring it up anymore.

Love

Resolving conflict doesn't mean you part ways. It means you forgive and value your time with the person or people involved.

As the tribe of Christ, we choose to accept people as they are. We do that because God meets us where we are. We give others room to make mistakes, and when they do, we love them through it.

"Hey, that hurt, didn't it?"

"Yeah."

"Alright, let's get up and try this again."

I'm going to hold that person's hand across the finish line. That's what we do. In all things, we love. When we approach a situation, we do it in love. When we bring the Word of God, we do it in love. We don't bring the Word to condemn. The Holy Spirit convicts, not us. If the heart behind our words or actions is not love, then we had better not say a thing. It's not our job. There's plenty of condemnation in the world. It shouldn't come from Christians.

Conclusion

There's going to be conflict in life, but when we join together in resolution, we are restored to go back out there. We are not to become cloistered, failing to reach into the world around us. That does no good. We are the salt of the earth. If we don't go into the world, how are people to find the hope they're looking for?

We come together to be with one another, to be fully accepted, to be loved and not judged. One of us can have an ugly day and we're going to say, "Come here. Hugs in." And our hearts are strengthened.

We all encounter conflict in relationships. We all struggle day-in and day-out. Conflict is not a bad thing. Sometimes conflict among us purifies the body, working out the imperfections. How we handle conflict and practice relationship in these places brings us all closer to the Lord...if we do it righteously. Maintain your integrity and set your boundaries.

> *Let the Lord judge the peoples. Vindicate me, Lord, according to my righteousness, according to my integrity, O Most High.*

> Psalm 7:8

> *I will never admit you are in the right; till I die, I will not deny my integrity.*

> Job 27:5

This scripture appears as Job's friends were coming to him, saying:

"Job, surely you screwed up."

"This disaster wouldn't have happened if you hadn't done this."

"Well, what about your kids? Didn't they do...?"

They are acting as persecutors, accusing him. His response is powerful: "No. I am innocent. Let me help you understand. I'm never going to accept that your lies are right. And I'm not going to curse God and die. I will uphold my integrity."

How do we defend against the lies of the enemy? We use the Word of God. But when your brother or sister comes and accuses you, you hold your tongue. You take it to the Father because He is your righteousness. He will defend you. Your character will speak more than your words ever will.

> *They sent their disciples to him along with the Herodians. "Teacher," they said, "we know that you are a man of integrity and that you teach the way of God in accordance with the truth. You aren't swayed by others, because you pay no attention to who they are.*

> Matthew 22:16

Maintain your integrity. Keep all doors of offense closed. Do not allow others to disrespect your boundaries. Don't show partialism by preferring one over another by allowing one to cross what another cannot. Do not speak ill of them. Bless them. In the workplace, co-workers may come to you wanting details or gossip. Do not participate. Go quietly without any noise. Don't become part of the problem, rather draw health in the solution. Be consistent in doing what is righteous and holy. The way you choose to resolve your conflict is a direct correlation to your character.

ANCESTRAL

IDENTITY

6

ANCESTRAL SEED

In the scriptures, God makes regular reference to the generational line of Israel-Abraham, Isaac, and Jacob. Why is that significant? It is because life comes through the seed, represented in our lives as our generational heritage. Blessing also comes through the generational line as part of our spiritual and physical inheritance. In the case of Israel, God was bringing mankind's redeemer through that bloodline, and he wanted to show the track record.

In this chapter, we will examine historical identifiers that appear in our generation history that contribute to our identity.

Seed

Jesus came as the seed. He is the pure lineage that came from heaven, the living sacrifice. When we surrender to him, we are grafted back in as sons and daughters of God and are glorified inside and out. Jesus redeemed the birthright, freeing us to love God, love others, resist the enemy, obey the Word, and live rightly.

As redeemed men and women, the spirit of Christ is within us. As our birthright, we carry the glory of the Lord. When the woman touched the hem of Jesus' garment and was healed, it was his glory reaching her. She caught the tangible glory of him through his garment. She reached in and caught hold of his under armor, the innermost being. He felt the virtue leave his body and she was healed. This is our inheritance. Christ Jesus is our seed; as we mature, we grow into his likeness. Therefore, our inheritance is that we ourselves are healed, and as we carry the glory of Jesus, others may be healed.

What was cursed when Adam and Eve fell? The seed was cursed because no one could partake of the Tree of Life, and there would be pain in childbearing. The land and livelihood were cursed because man would now be required to put his sweat into the land.

Consider the story of Job from the Old Testament. Where was he initially attacked? He was attacked in his seed—his children and his family line. Yes, his physical body was attacked, as was his land and livestock. That was his livelihood. But the vital attack came against his lineage—the lasting impact to the bloodline.

Bloodline

It was through Adam and Eve that God was going to send his seed, his only begotten Son. This is why it had to be a pure bloodline. This was at the forefront of God's mind when He told Adam to subdue the earth, take dominion over every living thing whether it creeps on the ground, flies in the air, or is in the sea. Why? Because he also told Adam and Eve to procreate, multiply and replenish the earth. The first command of subduing the earth was necessary to fulfill the second command of multiplying and replenishing. There needed to be a world for the generations arising from their seed. God's inheritance comes to us through the seed.

Bloodlines carry a history of past generations. Each bloodline tells a story and conveys an inheritance of blessing or cursing; oftentimes a blend of both. Knowing this, we need to call forth that which is in our bloodlines—even going back hundreds of generations—and let it flow through us.

This realization requires a broad scope of thinking. Some of us can likely recall our families back three or four generations, but try to recall ten generations of our heritage? It would likely guide us into different countries, into cultures and worldviews of which we have little knowledge or appreciation.

It was Aurelius Ambrose (c. 340-397), Bishop of Milan, that has been quoted as saying, "When in Rome, do as the Romans do." He was speaking to Monica of Hippo and her son, Augustine, about fasting on Saturdays. Paul echoes this sentiment in his letter to the Romans:

> *Accept the one whose faith is weak, without quarreling over disputable matters. One person's faith allows them to eat anything, but another, whose faith is weak, eats only vegetables. The one who eats everything must not treat with contempt the one who does not, and the one who does not eat everything must not judge the one who does, for God has accepted them.*

> Romans 14: 1-3

The land reflects certain customs and behaviors of the generations. Even Peter struggled with his own convictions when the Lord changed his mindset, in Acts 10. He had certain customs and beliefs that he had to shed in order to be effective in the land where he was. This was the dawning of a new era which would require him to abandon some of his judgments around his practiced traditions and customs of his land.

Most of my life was spent in the southeastern part of the United States, and as part of the heritage on the land, it was ingrained into my annual practice to prepare and eat collard greens (cabbage in Louisiana), and black eye peas to ensure health and prosperity for the new year. It was a tradition in my family and in the south, yet it was all superstition which is quite predominant in the south. After all, my health and prosperity come through Christ Jesus. I don't need an excuse to cook collard greens because I love them, but black-eyed peas are a different story. In recent years, I discovered that the reason that black-eyed peas were part of this tradition is due to Sherman coming through the southern towns plundering and burning his way through. They only food remaining was for the cows which remained in the silos. The cattle fed on black-eyed peas. Yes, it was the black-eyed peas that kept the cattle and owners alive, but they were reduced to essentially eat from the trough. When we memorialize battles, death, poverty, people, we set up strongholds in the land for generations. Every time, I fed my children black-eyed peas to commemorate health and greens for wealth, I was idolizing poverty and cancelling out faith in God's provision. It cancelled out any form of prosperity. When I broke that poverty spirit off of our generational line and repented for commemorating such a horror year after year, we began to see tremendous breakthrough in our finances and our health.

When we consider traditions and what is in the land, we think of the here and now. What was the custom for your generational line seven generations ago? Where were they from at that time? What about fifty generations ago? Have you traced your ancestors back that far to see what may have been your customs according to the land they were from, the time they lived in, and what governments and religions ruled that era? What were some of the characteristics of the land, or country during that time? Was it righteous or wicked?

What different religions might appear as we looked back into our generational lineage? Remember, there was no religion when there was only God. Naturally, it is in man's nature to worship something, so if people didn't worship God, they worshiped other things instead: physical objects or other spiritual entities. An important ramification of worship is that we align with whatever we worship, and through this alignment comes our inheritance. Our chief inheritance as Christians, then, is the governance of God as the creator and we as his children.

Part of this relationship is our inheritance of the land and the livelihood it produces. This is part of the blessing to Christ-ones when we were grafted into Christ, and everything of the Kingdom is ours. Nothing is withheld. God is no respecter of persons.

Religion

In the beginning...there was no religion. There was only God, and he is not religious. He's a spirit being, and we are created in his image and in likeness.

One Sunday morning, the Lord was talking to me about when Adam partook of the knowledge of the tree of good and evil. He showed me that Eve's glory didn't dim when she partook of the fruit. This is because Adam was her covering and they were one flesh: equal. Sin was not complete until Adam partook of the fruit. When he took the bite, it was done. God's glory on both of them began to fade, they saw they were naked, and they hid from God. When the glory diminished, Adam and Eve finally noticed the effects of what they had done. Once they saw that they were naked—uncovered of God's glory—and they were fearful and ashamed.

It's interesting to realize that Adam and Eve didn't know each other through nakedness, but only through their glorified identity. They didn't see their physical nature until after they partook of the fruit. God is going to ask you to abandon some of your religious beliefs because they do not allow his truths to thrive. Allow him to take you to the place he desired creation to be from the beginning in order for him to restore through you his kingdom on earth.

Abrahamic Blessing

In Genesis 17, God made a blood covenant with Abram and changed his name to Abraham through circumcision. This was a type and shadow of Jesus' bloodshed that brings us into covenant with God and represented through communion. What life and lineage do you bring through your righteousness? How does it affect the land? Why would it affect your livelihood? Let's step back a few chapters to see how it all fits together.

Genesis 12 calls Abram out of his father's land so the Lord can make Abram a great nation. He took with him his wife, nephew, and all possessions. God told Abram he would give this land to Abram's offspring; he would make him a great nation. While in the land, Abram acquired sheep, cattle, donkeys, camels, and servants. In chapter 13, we find out that God did, in fact, make Abram very wealthy with livestock, silver, and gold. Lot was also blessed. When Abram gave Lot his pick of the land, God further blessed Abram through his offspring in this land. Abram was generous in all his ways, faithful to the Lord and did as the Lord instructed.

The Lord was so pleased with Abram that in Genesis 15, he came to visit Abram in a vision. Now that Abram had stewarded his investment in the land, God was going to bring him an heir. Abram, believing the Lord, had righteousness credited toward him. When you take the Lord at his word, righteousness is accredited toward you. It divinely opens you up to the covenants of God. The Lord had given to him new land, blessed it, multiplied his possessions, and was now going to give him heirs through Abraham's seed. Could it be that your heirs represent the righteousness God credited you? Might *you* and your descendants represent the righteousness credited through others in your generational line? Your seed represents life and lineage.

Now, let's begin by focus primarily on three historical identifiers: the seed, land, and livelihood; that come through the Abrahamic blessing. It is the life and legacy of our seed. The seed not only comes through our generational line but is also transferred into the land. If I have family land, and the family grows and spreads out on it, it has an impact on subduing and compelling the land to produce. The same is true of our spiritual territory. In the scriptures, the livelihood of a family was seen in their livestock. The family's livelihood was affected by how much land and livestock they had. The blessings of growth and expansion left a legacy.

This is why Abraham's blessing involved an impartation of the land because God clearly defined those borders of the land—east, west, north, and south—and he talked about the additional territories that he was going to take.

Seed, Land, Livelihood

Seeds are made to be planted in the land, grow to maturity, and produce a harvest. If a seed is placed in the right environment, it will prosper. It is the law of nature, also referred to as a Kingdom Principle called *"the seed."* - If a seed is planted in the right conditions, then it will grow and produce.

The force that put your personal destiny in motion is *seed*. As a human being, you came into this world in your mother's womb—the result of a seed being formed there. As such, you were a seed within a seed bearer. You were a seed in an environment conducive to growth. Then you were separated and grew into a mature being capable of producing seed. Notice, however, that no faith is required for seed to grow. The cycle continues, regardless of your faith, due to Laws of Creation.

The Land—the physical world around us is a part of our natural environment. It partners with us to grow and produce seed. That is the purpose of the land. It was created to provide for creatures of the earth. As God's design, the land follows the same Kingdom Principles as do human beings (and all living creatures) regarding the seed. If man stewards the land, it will produce provisions. If it was created to be the provision for man, then it must be. If the land does not provide, then man has not stewarded it.

Indeed, it is from the collaboration of the land, seed, and healthily functioning in our gifts and talents that unlocks kingdom wealth to leaves behind a legacy of blessing through our birthright.

The land and waters provide the necessary environment for the seed to grow. Not only is there a gas exchange to allow us to breathe, but also provides us food and water while generating other resources needed for our habitation and livelihood (waterfalls, wind, oil, minerals).

I cannot create gold, but if I mine the minerals from the land, I now possess a resource of a valuable commodity. The land and I have teamed our resources, creating an ability to use gold to trade for something else or to set it aside to grow in wealth.

Likewise, I cannot make vegetables, yet I can plant seeds and wait for them to grow. Once the seeds produce vegetables, I can use the produce and set aside seed for the next planting. I can also sell some of the produce, store it or eat it. This is part of the same Kingdom Principle that I refer to as *"the livelihood."* If man will work the land and invest his time (seed), then it will yield a provision called livelihood, such as with the sower and the reaper. Your livelihood is linked to your identity. It propels you into your purpose and positions you for authority.

The Kingdom Principles of the seed, land, and livelihood is what we are going to explore more in-depth over the next few chapters, but it must be considered throughout the series. As you study these three components of covenant, remember to view them from the two-sided coin of the birthright and the blessing. As a child of God, the glory within you operates from both sides of the physical and spiritual parts of the birthright and the blessing as defined in the introduction.

7

LAND IDENTITY

Whether you have ever been to China or not, you can rest assured that once you step off the plane, you will be submerged into a Chinese culture. Everything is different, including their architecture, government, religion, and traditions. Their language is even assured to have its own slang or accentual sound depending on the region or major territory. The cultural anthropology of China, developed over hundreds of generations, determines this native group of human beings as Chinese. Therefore, the land of China reflects those who occupy it, and it will only take you a few moments to recognize the cultural differences between your country and theirs.

The Garden

God created Adam and placed him in the Garden of Eden to live. Notice, however, that God did not build Adam a home or cook him dinner, but instead, he gave him a garden with food, water, and even gold—everything he would need to prosper...almost. God saw that it was not good for man to be alone, so he provided a mate. Because the scriptures say that God knows a need before we ever think it, we can conclude that he knew Adam and Eve would need basic necessities to live and procreate. Therefore, everything they required for survival was provided on earth.

God used the earth's resources to create Adam from the dust and created Eve from the rib of Adam. This introduces the relationship between man and the land. From dust we were created and to the dust our bodies return. This is where the Kingdom Principles of the seed, land and livelihood originate—with the sower, the reaper or giver and receiver.

It was the law of the land to supply food and shelter for all created things. This is a depiction of the wheel-within-a-wheel relationship between God and the land, God and man, man and seed, man, and land. Man's *livelihood* is based on his obedience to do as God says regarding the seed and land, while the land obeys God to produce on behalf of man. Interestingly, the land's obedience is not a given. When the land does not follow the Kingdom Principle, it is cursed. In Mark 11, for example, Jesus passed by a fig tree and found it bare. Later in the day, he passed it again and saw that it was still bare, so he cursed the fig tree. It later withered and died.

Following this principle, we know that we are to cut off the roots to anything which does not produce fruit as God has commanded. We see this law in action when Adam and Eve disobey God's commands.

It was not God's intention for man to work the ground in toil or to experience pain in childbearing. These things are the consequences of wrong choices that led to disobedience. Because they were cursed for their disobedience, God had to cut off Adam and Eve from the Tree of Life. The pattern of this Kingdom Principle remains true throughout scripture. Some examples from the Old Testament are found in the story of Job, Abraham, Isaac, Jacob, David, and Solomon. In the New Testament, we see these principles in the lives of Jesus and his disciples.

Each of the twelve tribes of Israel was indicative of a particular blessing unique to that tribe. A blessing was spoken over each son of Israel. It flowed to his section of land and the nation that flowed from him. As that tribe walked into its identity, so did the land. The land now became the identity of that tribe.

Imagine you are headed to a specific address. You recognize the street, city and nation, the particular place, and the fact that a friend lives there. But when you get there, you notice something further. The land is hers. It echoes her sound and language. Because she is a godly woman, when you look at her home, it gives forth the presence of God. The grandeur of the house or the lack thereof doesn't matter. It could be a mansion or a hovel. Yet, it will radiate God's Spirit if the inhabitants are aligned with God.

If you have a $500 car or a $50,000 car, it still reflects Jesus when you steward it well. If all you can afford right now is a $500 car, thank God for that $500 car and appreciate its ability to transport you from point A to point B. Take care of it as a gift from God.

Think about how others may see you. You might have a little fish symbol on your car to show you are a Christian, but are you cutting people off in traffic? Are you flipping them the universal sign language of unity? We are to reflect God's language in everything over which we have been given stewardship. For example, every property I've ever owned has been prayed over and staked off. The properties are in the protective custody of Jesus, and the love language of God has been released over them, resulting in our present tenants having no desire to vacate. (That is a miracle!) We value the home where they reside. Likewise, they demonstrate appreciation for what we own to steward it well by taking good care of the property and paying rent on time. We demonstrate our appreciation of them by readily responding to any requests or concerns they share. We partner together in relationship to bring about the best for us all and the land.

Now, that doesn't mean challenges never happen. But being a good steward to all that God has given me helps create an atmosphere for others to partner in the stewardship.

Remember Jesus' parable of the master who gave out talents to his servants. To one he gave one talent. To another servant, he gave five talents. To a third servant, he gave ten talents. Unfortunately, the first servant buried his talents in the ground instead of investing (and risking) his master's money. The master was giving each one an opportunity to prove themselves. *OK, this is it. I'm going to give you this talent. But I'm watching to see what you do with this. And it's going to measure where we go from here.*

The master was essentially drawing the line in the sand for his servants just as God did with the Israelites. *You're either going to enter in now, to a new dimension of understanding, a new dimension of the promise, or you're going to stay where you've always been. But I'm giving you the opportunity to walk into a new level of authority.* But the first servant didn't recognize the opportunity, and he didn't take possession of a new place.

When it came time to give an account, the servant used all his excuses as though they were going to measure up. But his excuses didn't measure up with his master, and our excuses don't measure up with God. He couldn't care less about our excuses. He has heard them all.

Justification is the way we rationalize a bad choice. Sometimes we need to listen to our own excuses. If others were coming at you with the same excuses, would you believe them? You'd probably say: "Why don't you just tell me you don't want to do it." God is the same way. He just wants us to tell him, "This is my hang-up. This is where I'm struggling. I know you want me to take this talent and multiply it, but I'm afraid. I've been told to multiply this talent Lord, but I haven't been shown how to do that. I don't know if I'm even worthy of having this talent." Justification is not the answer. Truth is.

Be real with God. He already knows you better than you know yourself. We need to confront our inhibitions. We need to confront those thoughts and the mixed language that comes out of our mouth. As we realize the things we are saying and their effect on our lives, we can put them to death and move on. When we air out our excuses, we can hear how ridiculous they are. *Did I just say that? That's absurd. Where did that come from? Where's the root of that?*

Our proper response must always go back to God's Word and his perspective: *God, your love language and your Word says these things about who I am. It says you are these things.* His language reproduces the promise. This is his relationship with man and the land; indeed, all of his creation. It's up to us to step into it. We do it through obedience. We do it by getting into the Word and declaring the Word of our lives instead of those pestering lies that we keep telling ourselves.

God's not buying our excuses. Why are we?

> *He loves righteousness and justice; the earth is full of the lovingkindness of the Lord.*

> Psalm 33:5 NASB

This scripture describes the sound that the earth made before sin entered the world—one of loving-kindness. Can you imagine what loving-kindness sounds like? A sweet lullaby? Tranquil, peaceful, beautiful? That's what the earth sounds like. That's our inheritance.

As we take our dominion in the land, a new sound is released from the earth. Not the groaning of pain, but joyful worship and serenity. It's a beautiful sound because God is beauty. As his sound is released in the earth, it exudes life.

As we release God's sound in the earth, we actually become younger. Because his Word is life-giving, our years are unwound as it flows through us. Aging is the process of death. If God is life-giving, then what is death? I don't mean to suggest that we will not die. We will. But we will not feel the pain of that transition.

O death, where is thy sting? O grave, where is thy victory?

1 Corinthians 15:55 KJV

What can I do in a 40-year-old body that I can't do in a 120-year-old body? I can be more effective, physically. Now, the spiritual aspect is still present. It's still moving and rolling and building and growing. But when my physical body comes into alignment with what my spirit has to fulfill on the earth, how much more can be accomplished?

If I'm releasing curses over my land—if I'm not in a right state of mind or if I keep speaking anything other than the language of love over my land—what does that do? "The herd's just not looking good this year. They're scrawny, they're not fat enough. They've all lost babies in the cold. We'll never get a decent price at market. I reckon we'll never see rain."

Negativity breeds negativity. However, as owner, I'm the authoritative spokesperson for the tribe that occupies that land. Therefore, I am the one releasing words of blessing or cursing over it. My sound is released and becomes one with the land.

Everything is one with God; it is all his creation. There's a constant movement of the sound back and forth, and this affects what happens in the land. The cow gets sick because I'm speaking death over it. Or all the cows have twins, and they win blue medals because I am speaking blessings and stewarding the herd. Our words are having a wide-ranging and direct impartation into the land and the fruit of that land. Our livelihood is affected by our words. As we release it, so is it.

> *For the mouth speaks what the heart is full of.*

> Matthew 12:34

If it's not life, it's going to be death. Out of the mouth comes blessings and curses. Sometimes we just need to shut our mouths, because honestly, our words don't compare to God's words. Sometimes we just need to say, "God, what are you saying about this?"

> *For the earth is the Lord's, and the fulness thereof.*

> I Corinthians 10:26 KJV

Yes, the earth is the Lord's, but we are heirs with Christ. He is within us, and we now take ownership in the earth just as Adam and Eve were originally commissioned to do.

So, let's test this logic. If I have a home, and I have children that live in my home, do they have partial ownership in that home with me? Yes, they do. They still have to go by the rules set by the authority in the home (the homeowner), but yes, everything that is within that home is equally theirs. They use the same rooms I do. They use the appliances, look out the windows, even take part in cleaning. I don't delineate ownership by saying: "This particular room is mine; stay out."

Of course, I realize this is a choice I made. Some families do section off living areas and restrict their children's access. In my case, however, I reasoned that the home was my children's sanctuary, and therefore, there would be no areas off-limits to them. And I'm not going to own anything that is so valuable to me that if they should break it, I'm going to have a fit. Stuff happens. (That's why I own a broom and a dustpan.) At the same time, I am not constantly following the children around waiting for them to break something. They have the freedom to move about within the house freely.

God gives us room to move about freely in all that he made. He allows us the freedom to exercise who we are and what we do. The scripture gives us clear lines about our responsibilities as we live together with him, and we have full access. When we make a mess, we repent, and he comes alongside us to clean it up together.

This concept of moving freely in our identity is in the core of who I am. Have you ever been in a home, school, workplace, or ministry where you did not have the freedom to be you? I have had jobs where my gifts and talents were not utilized because I was not politically positioned to exercise fully in my identity. An example of this is where I have been in churches where only pastors are allowed to do certain things. People within the church were only permitted leadership if they were the largest givers or had certain family affiliations. We have each been assigned our talents to move and use freely for the Kingdom of God.

The inheritance of God does not discriminate. It is for everyone. And since it is freely given, we can freely distribute it. Your gifts and callings come from God, and they are irrevocable. Through the blood of Jesus Christ, all that God has created is yours. He established you before the foundation of the world to be you, just as you are. As we grow in relationship with him, we gain a better understanding of the freedom we have in him. When we have a word from God that needs to be released, we have the freedom in Christ to share that word. No authority can take that from us. Now, there are times and seasons that we have to sit on something and birth it out but wait upon the Lord. He will make the provision for you just like it says in Habakkuk 2:2-3. The question is timing: Is it for the whole body now? Or are they being prepared to receive it at a later time?

When we hold on to the negativity of our language, allowing ourselves to be vain and proud, we soon find that there's a price for that. Jesus already paid the price. But when we try to overstep his value, there's going to be a fall. And it's going to mean more than skinned knees. The value of this inheritance is priceless. But it is free for you.

The earth is defiled by its people; they have disobeyed the laws,
violated the statutes and broken the everlasting covenant.

Isaiah 24:5

Traveling to certain areas of the country or the world, it's easy to see what's important to the local population. Some people and cultures obviously value the land and others don't. Some people just don't know how. Like the servant with one talent, he might not have known what to do with a talent.

Judgment

One of the roles of the body of Christ is to bring the knowledge of God to others. We need to partner with the Holy Spirit, however, to know what knowledge needs to be imparted to help people better steward the land. We have to teach them through a spirit of love because judgment never wins.

Judgment is, by divine nature, a penalty of death. That's why we were not supposed to partake of the tree of the knowledge of good and evil, because all-knowing, pure, and unadulterated knowledge and wisdom is within God. But when we're in sin, such knowledge is contaminated and therefore brings death.

Judgment is death. Yet, God's judgment brings life because life is freely given through repentance. Man took part of the judgment that meant death, not knowing what it would mean. God said, "You must not eat from the tree of the knowledge of good and evil, for when you eat from it you will certainly die" (Genesis 2:17). God spoke it, but man didn't understand the fullness of the Word until it was too late. God's Word is designed to give us testimony so that we will not disobey any longer.

In Jesus, we come under God's full redemptive power and receive our full inheritance through the gift of repentance. From this vantage point, we can look and see that the earth is beautiful. The earth is still the Lord's, and we can be better stewards of it. We can be more accountable for what is released in the earth. It's tied to our sound, to that which we release.

Why is the earth so attached to our sound and not our actions? Because our body follows the direction of the mind, and our mind follows our sound. As our mind thinks, so it is. This principle not only affects our lives and what we do, but it also has consequences in the physical and in the land.

Through our prayers, God heals more than just our lives. He heals our land.

> *If my people, who are called by my name, will humble themselves and pray and seek my face and turn from their wicked ways, then I will hear from heaven, and I will forgive their sin and will heal their land.*

2 Chronicles 7:14

What are you releasing in your land? What are you saying about your inheritance? The choice is clear. You're either giving life to your inheritance or you're killing it. It's that simple. There's no in-between.

> *The increase from the land is taken by all; the king himself profits from the fields.*

Ecclesiastes 5:9

Homeward Bound

Jesus himself found comfort in the land. Where did he go in troubled times? When He pulled himself away into seclusion, he went to the mountains or a garden. He found peace in the land and tarried there with the Lord.

Where do you go when you're seeking refuge? Do you take a drive to the country? Do you go to the gym? Do you go home? Our immediate family calls two places home: Tennessee and South Carolina. I cherish them both for different things that are dear to me. But when I need to break away, I go to my ancestral lands in South Carolina.

Our legacy is what results from the inherited land. It's the land that I'm known by for generations. It's my peaceful place. It's the place that I visit in my dreams when I'm having a nighttime encounter with God.

That land speaks to me. My spirit is one with that land. I can tell you what's on that land, some of it good and some of it bad. But every time I go,

I have a purpose in mind. And it's not just to restore my innermost self, but also to reestablish a right standing in the land while I'm there. It is still mine. It is still my inheritance. We are served by the land. It produces a yield, a livelihood, and a sanctuary for us. It inhabits our blessings from God.

When you leave work for the day, where do you want to go? Home. Why? Because it's yours. It is familiar. You can stay with a friend; you can stay with a loved one for months. But the heart longs to be home.

We moved so much when our family was young; both from serving in ministry and my husband's work in banking. We should have just gone into the military; we would have moved less. Our kids would wonder, "Mom, where do we call home? We've known so many homes." I would answer, "Home is where your stuff is."

We have an identity in our possessions. There's a reason we purchase and own things. Our identity is reflected through those things. What's left of us if we don't have those things? The Lord intended for us to have land. It gives us everything we need. Our possessions represent the land and its yield.

My grandfather talked about the value of land. You can make anything out of land, as long as you have land and put your hand to it. If you put your focused intention to it, you're going to have a yield. If you speak death over it, it's going to be desolate and dry. Your yield is what you put into it.

The legacy of the land is your inheritance. Your legacy will come through the way you steward it. It's up to us how we multiply it. It doesn't matter if you have an eighth of an acre or 800 acres, metaphorically speaking. Whatever you sow into that land, it will produce a yield for you. This is the covenantal principle of God's kingdom as an heir in Christ.

This is a provision of God. All you have to do is recognize that you hold the key...and that key looks very much like a tongue. Take your words and you unlock life through the land. Your tongue becomes a key having total access to the Kingdom of Heaven.

So, as you look around yourself, take an account of your land. Recognize what God has given you through the conventual inheritance? This is now your territory. Steward it well.

8

KINGS AND PRIESTS

In studying our inheritance—our land, our generational line, and our future—we also looked at the Abrahamic blessing. But ultimately, as believers in Christ, we walk in new authority. An activation occurs when we surrender to Jesus. It releases a new work in us—an identity related to the kings and priests that we are.

> *But you are a chosen people, a royal priesthood, a holy nation, God's special possession, that you may declare the praises of him who called you out of darkness into his wonderful light.*

1 Peter 2:9

Kings and Priests

This identity of kings and priests is part of the blessing overflow from the Father demonstrated in our livelihood. Being born again in Christ brings the birthright blessing of eternal life. We become co-heirs and co-laborers with Christ. This is the gift of grace. The abundant blessing comes as we continue to live righteously in our relationship with the Lord. This requires discipline and perseverance. It is through our active participation in righteousness that the overflow comes, the blessing of livelihood. Even when we mess up, we are given new opportunities to prove we are capable of possessing the keys to the kingdom. This is his mercy.

The first historical example of a king and priest that we see in scripture is Melchizedek. He was a king residing on the east side of the Jordan River when a war broke out over Abraham's nephew, Lot. Lot had moved to the east side of Jordan and settled around Sodom and Gomorrah. Unfortunately, some other kings invaded this region, took Lot prisoner, and stole all his possessions.

Word of Lot's plight got back to Abraham, and he went to get Lot out of prison and to take back all that was stolen. Now, Abraham did not have an army, so he took his household and servants with him—that's all he had. But he left immediately to rescue his kinsman. And as he was returning from the defeat of the kings, King Melchizedek met him with bread and wine and spoke a blessing on him.

> *Blessed be Abram by God Most High,*
>
> *Creator of heaven and earth.*
>
> *And praise be to God Most High,*
>
> *who delivered your enemies into your hand.*
>
> Genesis 14:19-20

In so doing, Melchizedek was acting as a priest, offering a ceremonial blessing for Abraham to honor him and to give reverence to what the Lord had done. In response, Abraham gave Melchizedek a tithe—a tenth of everything.

Abraham's approach was simple. He'd sworn an oath to God, acted honorably, and returned rejoicing: *Here God, I'm alive today because of you. You saved my nephew. Because you've saved my family. I'm going to give you an offering.* He gave a tithe to Melchizedek, recognizing the favor of God upon his life and Melchizedek's place as God's king and priest.

Jesus came as a king and priest—*the* King of Kings and High Priest. But he wasn't immediately recognized as such. He walked among men. He ate and slept and worked among the common people. It wasn't until after he ascended that people understood his position.

> *For it is clear that our Lord descended from Judah, and in regard to that tribe Moses said nothing about priests. And what we have said is even more clear if another priest like Melchizedek appears, one who has become a priest not on the basis of a regulation as to his ancestry but on the basis of the power of an indestructible life.*

For it is declared: "You are a priest forever, in the order of Melchizedek."

Hebrews 7:14-17

Before the King

Historically, there were certain times of the year when people would say: "The king is in the field." This marked a time when they could go out and approach the king with their petitions. In the Old Testament, before Queen Esther could enter the king's throne room, she had to wait for him to acknowledge her. He would signal whether she could enter or not. And because she pleased him, he allowed her to enter.

Likewise, we petition the Lord when he is approachable. The blessing that comes from being kings and priests, however, is that we actually represent God's royalty. Therefore, we have those components of rulership. We have a kingdom that we are ruling until Jesus returns.

Consider Joseph from the book of Genesis. He was second in command to Pharaoh of Egypt and bore a signet ring representing Pharaoh's authority. Whatever he said was the law, the same as Pharaoh's word.

As believers in Christ, we have that same ability within us. Although we are children of God, we are also joint heirs with Jesus. We are placed beside him in heaven. As we go forth in our rulership, we exercise our rights as joint heirs with Christ, understanding our authority in him. When he returns again, he will establish his earthly kingdom in Jerusalem, in the holy city. We will reign with him in other kingdoms as they are given to us.

In the Old Testament, similar blessings came upon the 12 sons of Jacob. Not only was each man a son of Jacob, but each son became a nation—a tribe of Israel—and each nation was represented in the 12 stones embedded in the breastplate of the high priest. The high priest had to be purified before he went into the heart of the temple—the Holy of Holies. In his preparation, he would don the priestly breastplate bearing the 12 stones representing the 12 nations of Israel, and the government of God.

As believers in Christ, we have the mark of God on our heads, and we bear the breastplate of righteousness that is in Christ Jesus. Just as the Old Testament priests had to prepare themselves before entering the presence of God in the temple, as kings today, there are things around us that must be prepared before we enter God's presence. Honor begets honor. Therefore, preparedness honors the king. But as priests, we go in as the sacrifice—the offering. Esther spent a year of purifying before she was ever presented to the king. Of course, Esther served a pagan king. Our king is Jesus Christ. As the bride of Christ, we prepare to enter his presence by anointing ourselves with the oils and fragrance of worship. When we are ready, we are able to enter the Holy of Holies as priests.

Because priests were the only ones who could enter the Holy of Holies, they represented the bride of Christ. Today, we are of the lineage of kings and priests from Melchizedek to Jesus. When Jesus returns, he will be king of kings. Yes, we will be kings, but He will be *the* King, *the* Lord of lords.

The Gifts as Kings and Priests

In finalizing our study of the ancestral identifiers, we will examine the redemptive gifts, the governmental gifts, and the manifestation gifts.

Kings and priests share an authoritative relationship in governmental roles. Priests issue the law and kings execute it. Priests study the law and spend time with the Lord. They meet with the prophets, the teachers, the scribes (historians) and form a plan. Then the priests go before the kings, and they consult one another on the meaning of the law and how it should be applied. This is how God's government functions. Note that it is a government, not a religion. God is not religious.

The first priest on earth was Adam. He was the authority on earth, appointed by God. Recall from our previous discussion that there was no diminishing of their glory when Eve took of the forbidden fruit. This is because God made a provision through Adam. Eve continued to bear the glory through her covenant relationship with Adam as long as Adam was in right relationship with God. If, instead of also taking of the fruit, Adam would have offered sacrifice to God, Eve would have been forgiven and there would have been no judgment or curse. Why? Because Adam was the priest of his family. He was the one who governed and provided protection. God's approach to Adam was simple: *Hey, I'm giving you the keys. I want you to rule the earth, subdue it, appropriate all these things I'm giving to you. You've got this. Do what you need to do. But remember, don't touch this tree. This tree is mine.*

The tree of the knowledge of good and evil belonged to God. It was the portion of the garden that he withheld. Today, there are also things that God withholds. Even though believers have free reign of the entire earth, there are still portions that belong strictly to the Lord, and we are not to touch them. We are not to steal from them. We have no part of them.

Abraham understood this, which is why he brought his offering before the Lord through the priest Melchizedek. It was as if he was saying: *I recognize all of this is yours, Lord. But here's the portion that you've asked of me, Lord God.* Abraham honored the Lord in that moment with Melchizedek. Adam, on the other hand, failed to do so when he partook of the forbidden fruit. He failed to respect God's boundaries. That's when the glory on both him and Eve diminished. Instead of offering a sacrifice, there was only disobedience without repentance.

Priests in the Home

Consider the priests today. My husband is the priest of our home. As such, he serves a vital role in the government of God in our family. It is critical that the family respect the husband's role.

I learned this lesson in our marriage when my husband made an innocent, yet costly mistake. To his credit (and God's favor) he did it with the right heart. He didn't have a hidden agenda. He honestly thought, in his heart of hearts, that he was making the right decision. But the entire time he was putting the plan in motion, I was praying: "My God, you know that's not what we're supposed to do. But what do I do?" And God said, "Honor your husband. As long as you honor him, there will not be a judgment against you."

I learned in that moment that whatever method I may have used to get him on my side, it would have been the wrong thing because the Lord was using it as a teaching moment. In the end, we did not suffer a curse or a judgment, and everything worked out for the best. Why? Because my husband's heart was in the right place, and so was mine. I learned that, as long as he's got the right heart for his family, God's going to put us wherever we're supposed to be, whenever we're supposed to be there.

Now, that doesn't mean we won't learn lessons. Yes, our family learned from that episode. Further, my husband and I know how to work together. We are a team. However, in *this* incident, God was letting my husband err for a reason, and I had to stand down.

We need to understand where our alignment is, and we need to honor our alignment. This is why scripture says: "*Husbands, love your wives, just as Christ loved the church and gave himself up for her*" (Ephesians 5:25). Husbands are not to lord over their wives, but to embrace them and keep them safe from judgment, leading them to walk rightly.

Consider Job's wife from the Old Testament. At the height of his suffering, she uttered her infamous invective: "*Are you still maintaining your integrity? Curse God and die!*" (Job 2:9). Notice, however, that she didn't come out and curse God herself. Instead, she stayed under her husband's priesthood and told him to do it. Ironically, because Job didn't do what she said and curse God through his trials, he was blessed. Because their covenant was recognized by God, she shared in his blessing. If Job had followed her advice, the consequences would have cost her severely. She would have been without a husband, a family, a home, servants, with nothing of the remnant that God used to multiply Job's blessings.

When Job's trials were ended, he had his home, his wife and four servants. He lost his children and most of the servants. Out of the debris of what remained, God brought about more because Job remained a righteous man in his right perspective for the salvation of his home. Remember, it was Job who was making the sacrifices for his children, out of fear they would sin against God.

The priesthood keeps us covered, and we need to honor that. We may not always agree, but we can agree to disagree, right? Yes, there will occasionally be inner conflict. But as long as we stay in right relationship as priests and under our priesthood, we will be spared a harsh discipline, a judgment, or a curse. It is when we rebel against our covering that we experience difficult consequences.

The same thing with our kings. We have to honor our kings. We may not agree with them, but we should not talk against them. There will always be things that we don't like or agree with. However, we need to put our feelings on the altar and surrender them to God. Whatever emerges from sacrifice to God is what we should act upon, but again, with reverence. *"Wives, submit yourselves to your own husbands as you do to the Lord"* (Ephesians 5:22). Jesus is our husbandry, and we need to understand that He has our best interests at heart. And he is the only thing saving us from a judgment of death. It is nothing in us. *"For it is by grace you have been saved, through faith—and this is not from yourselves, it is the gift of God—not by works, so that no one can boast"* (Ephesians 2:8-9).

When the priests enter the Holy of Holies, they are wearing the breastplate that reflects the 12 tribes of Israel. These tribes came from the 12 sons of Jacob, and they represent the government of God. They are the 12 tribes in the land and the 12 nations of resources.

They further represent the 12 months contained within the government of the times and seasons, and they are also the 12 living stones which are represented in the New Testament for the disciples.

In addition, if you put the seven redemptive gifts with the fivefold governmental gifts, you will have a total of 12 gifts. These must be combined to work together because they represent the complete governmental body of Christ—his bride.

These gifts overlap and are to be used interchangeably. We are to exercise all 12 gifts so we will become fluid in their operation. We are all fitly joined together. Where I lack, you have abundance. Where you lack, I have abundance. As Christ-ones, our strength is made in him as we work together in love.

Governmental Gifts

As kings and priests, we are to rule and take dominion in Jesus' name. When we do this, we become part of the governmental legislation of God. Let's look at some different ways this happens. One of the ways we govern is through the five governmental gifts listed in Ephesians.

> *So, Christ himself gave the apostles, the prophets, the evangelists, the pastors and teachers, to equip his people for works of service, so that the body of Christ may be built up until we all reach unity in the faith and in the knowledge of the Son of God and become mature, attaining to the whole measure of the fullness of Christ.*

Ephesians 4:11-13

Although the gifts have distinct names, they are intertwined. We call them fivefold gifts, offices or anointings, but in reality, they are governmental gifts. Interestingly, governmental gifts reside in us but remain dormant until we are born again. When we come to Christ Jesus, these gifts rise within us, and we begin to operate as God designed us.

Although a particular governmental gift may be distinctive because of your personality type and redemptive gift, do not stifle any of the gifts as you move in the Spirit. More than one gift can be present and operational. In addition, each gift will manifest in different ways depending on the circumstances, the state of the people involved, and the particular move of God. (Yes, God varies in his approach.)

In all things, we must understand that our governmental gifts are essentially authority. They are mantles of authority that are awakened in us when we come into the fullness of Christ Jesus, being filled with his Spirit. When this occurs, our identities shift and are catapulted into something new and beautiful.

Remember, we have all five of these gifts, but we may not move in all five of those at the same time. Personally, I'm much better teaching believers than I am reaching out to those who have yet to make a commitment to

Christ. This is why I tend to operate as a teacher, but I can operate as an evangelist when God leads. It's slightly out of my element, but within reach of governmental gifts. Part of my difficulty is that I don't hold the office of an evangelist or teacher. I can move in either, even though they are not my office.

Here are the five governmental gifts in greater detail.

Apostles

Yes, apostles are for today. The church was still adding apostles after Jesus left the earth, and he never said "Stop!" The word *apostle* means *to go out, to be sent*. Most people believe that we still have missionaries. So, what qualifies a missionary? To be sent. To go out. And that is the main quality of an apostle.

My husband and I are not from our present locale. We were sent here. We knew that there was a spiritual assignment that we could not activate where we were living, it took being sent to put the assignment in motion in order to release it. That is the apostolic gift at work.

Apostles are also equippers. They are the dream awakeners. They see a vision, share it with you, and suddenly you now see it. They can create an experience and invite you into it in such a way that you are ready to run with it. Likewise, they can see the destiny within you. The apostle's main concern is moving the body of Christ toward the purposes of God, and they motivate others to do so by pursuing their destiny in Christ.

The apostle asks these things:

- Who are you?
- What are you called to do?
- If you don't know what you are called to, why not?
- How can we get you there?

The apostle wants you to live out your calling because there's more to you than meets the eye—yours or anybody else's.

When we walk into our governmental roles, we became super beings because we have both kings and priests within us—a lineage reaching all the way back to Adam. As we excel in the purposes of God, we release God's glory on earth, to fill it and subdue it and to have dominion until Jesus returns. And then when he returns, guess what? We're going to do the same thing. We're going to fill it and subdue it because we have our portion and we've stewarded it well.

Following Jesus and cultivating the growth of the kingdom is what drives apostles.

- How can we grow?
- How can we mature?
- How can we advance?
- How can we fulfill what we've been sent here to do?

Now, every gift of God has a downside—the consequences of taking our eyes off the Lord and starting to operate on our own. Even if our motives are good, we can go astray by thinking that it's all up to us. (That's almost as bad as thinking it's all up to God.)

The downside of the apostolic gift is that we can become too focused on production and get caught up in the business of running and promoting things, possessed of our vision for the sake of our vision. We need to understand that the governmental gifts are to be proportionate to the rest of our lives. In a word: balance. This is especially true of the apostolic gifting because of the great responsibilities it entails.

For my part, there are still things I want to fulfill in ministry. But I also want to have relationships. I want to have quiet time. I want to have leisure time. I want to have family time. I want to write more books. My gifting has to be in proportion to all that God has put in my heart. If I allow a single vision to take over everything, then it isn't a pleasure anymore. I'm not operating from the overflow of a full heart, but instead am bearing a loathsome burden in the spirit of religious obligation. Sure, we can ask God to take it from us and do it himself, but that's now how we are supposed to operate. We've been given our assignments; therefore, we must carry them out.

Apostles typically function in finite projects, without abandoning the infinite whole. It's just part of their makeup. When they see a particular vision being fulfilled, they're ready to have others step in and take over their role in it while they move on to the next vision. They will go to a new territory and expand the cultivating and growth of the kingdom of God. That's what they're supposed to do. If they're not moving, then they are not fulfilling the vision. Without frequent motion and often frequent change, the vision that's been imparted to apostles grows stagnant and the body of Christ becomes moribund.

Prophets

The prophet's governmental role functions like the heart—the emotional and spiritual epicenter of a living being. Prophets show us where we've been and where we are going. Unlike the apostle, whose focus is on where we're supposed to be, the prophet's message is more like this: *Well, we came from here, remember? Let's look at where we've been. We're tracking well.*

Prophets function like a conscience. They offer the plumb line that keeps us in balance. They ensure that we are walking hand in hand with God. If we get off course, they're the first to point it out, along with details of how we got off course, where we really should be and the consequences of not heeding their word by getting back on course sooner than later. They hold us accountable to walk with God, not in our own ways but in his ways.

King David found this out the hard way when the prophet Nathan confronted him over his affair with Bathsheba and the subsequent murder of her husband: "'You are the man!'...Then David said to Nathan, "I have sinned against the Lord.'" (2 Samuel 12:7, 13).

Personally, I can get easily sidetracked with what I want, even if it's from a good heart—especially if it's from a good heart, because it's harder to see through well-intentioned motives. But oftentimes what I want isn't going to fulfill God's vision. The prophet is going to hold me accountable to God's mandate. *Are you sure? Are you sure that's what God's saying? Let's check this out.*

Prophets have a spirit-filled lifestyle, and they participate in God's new age. If we are going to move forward in fulfilling God's purposes—if we are going to move into the Promised Land—we've got to walk closely with God. We can't keep dabbling in idolatry. We can't put our gold in the fire and watch it turn into a calf idol. We've got to eschew our wicked ways. The prophets are the ones who will call us out on our misdeeds. *No, we can't tolerate that here. You can no longer talk like that anymore. You're held to a different kind of accountability now; you're not just looking out for you and your own. Now you're in a company of truths. And so what you do and what you say happens to everyone here.*

We all bear the same name. That's God's name: Jesus Christ.

The downside of the prophetic gift is that prophets can be task-oriented, black-and-white in their view of things. So, it's difficult for them to acknowledge goodness and give it back, to bless people where they are. Because they're looking at the heart, they tend to see a particular vision or purpose in all its purity. Yes, a vision needs to be accurate and complete, but prophets can forget how to live in the real world with imperfect but good-hearted people. Prophets are driven to find spirit-formed people, those in whom the spirit is resonating, and once found, to draw them out and compel them to live a righteous and holy lifestyle.

Prophets are purists, and they don't get invited to many social functions.

Evangelist

Evangelists reach people where they are. They tend to be storytellers; they have a quip and an antidote for everything. Their nature makes them relatable to people. They talk to everyone, so they have more experiences than most. Personally, if I don't talk to five people in a day, I'm going to go home and say it's been a great day—I got a lot done. But an evangelist is going to talk to every person they encounter. They are going to know how everyone's day went, what's on their mind; they might hear a dozen stories but they're all going to be wonderful.

The evangelist's focal concern is incarnating the good news. *Let me tell you, Jesus is the reason for the season. Let me tell you, he paid it all and he'll pay it all for you.*

Joy exudes from them. It's contagious. People want to be around them all the time. Evangelists draw people, and that drawing compels change. They are people of welcome; they are change agents. They are the gatherers. They are the warm person you can always go to because they love on you even if you smell like something that should've stayed outside. They see beyond your faults and your temporary distresses. It doesn't matter if you've not showered in three weeks. They don't care. They love you because they see you not your circumstances, but *you*. They see your life was designed to know Jesus so your time here on earth is well spent.

Their arms offer love and hospitality where everybody's welcome, nobody is turned down. Their homes, families and lives are open to everybody. They want to bless everyone they come in contact with. You know when you've encountered this gift because you're going to feel like a million bucks when you are in that presence. You're going to feel the value of who you are. Evangelists fully demonstrate the love of Jesus.

The best salesmen in the commercial world are evangelists. They can tend to become competitive. On the downside, evangelists can be egocentric if they're operating incorrectly in their gifts. They can slip into becoming entertainers or place upon themselves a sense of false responsibility. They get really frustrated that everyone doesn't tell people about Jesus or the power of his blood.

Pastor

A pastor is a soul healer. He sees wounded emotions and afflictions making a way for inner healing and deliverance. They mend the brokenhearted, set the main course and equip people to finish the race. They shepherd God's sheep and give them the tools to mend the broken places in their lives. They work to prevent people from injuring themselves and others.

Such inner healing cannot be neglected. There's a time that we reflect, look inward and take care of our issues. Then we go back out. We can't spend our whole lives mending our wounds. At some point, we have to get back up and do it all over again. But neither can we ignore its need forever.

Pastors help the body of Christ get their wounds healed and become reconciled so that we can move together as a unified force.

When we are truly healed, there are no more wounds of the heart because we no longer wound others. Further, we understand the wounds that we've overcome, and we're healthier for it. Like all works of God, when healing is complete in us, we want other people to be healed. Sometimes the pastor's role is to broker the introduction between a broken person and the healer God because often the wounded person is the last to see their wounds.

Unfortunately, pastors can become battered and wounded themselves. They will either overextend themselves, fail to evaluate and deal with their own soul-issues or become a target themselves for other wounded people to inflict pain upon.

The first thing to understand is that wounded people tend to wound other people. If you extend your hand toward an injured dog, that dog is likely to bite you not because of anything you did, but because that dog is in pain and thinks you're going to hurt it. Who knows? You might? Wounded people unknowingly and sometimes knowingly inject their negative spirit into whoever tries to help them. Pastors often return from such encounters drained and hopeless, even when the wounded person received healing.

Because they have a heart of caring for God's people, pastors don't always know when to pull back from the wounded person they are trying to help. Making things worse, when they are repeatedly hurt, they can develop a tough exterior, thinking that this will protect them. Like all thick skins, however, it also keeps out well-intentioned people. Sometimes, pastors are the hardest people to relate to on a personal level. They either want to fix people, or they are retreating to recover from the wounds of doing so.

The second factor is that when a pastor deals with intimate things—the innermost parts of human lives—they can easily get drawn into the conflicting sides present in any complex issue. When the conflict involves their flock, they might become downright defensive, unconsciously taking sides when they should remain objective. Sometimes, the call to lead others out of their pain can create a codependency. This is extremely hazardous. The pastoral position of soul-healer includes soul-confronter. Tough issues must be faced and addressed. When others avoid facing the truth and a blunt confrontation is necessary, the pastor must be ready. (That is often when they call in a prophet for backup.)

Add to this the necessary level of secrecy required of pastors when sensitive soul-issues are aired out, and you have a man or woman who has no one bare to *their* soul to when the ministering is done. A pastor's first responsibility, before ever caring for the flock, is to care for themselves and their family. When these priorities are reversed, things go awry quickly.

Teacher

A teacher is the light-giver, the one to speak a word over you when you need it. When you're going through difficulties and you don't know where to turn, call the teacher. They may or may not give you empathy—it depends on the teacher—but they will give you the tools you need to fight your way out of the trenches. We need teachers; not only do they know the Word, but they've also proven it by living it.

The teacher's main focus is shaped by sacred text. If our lives do not reflect God's Word, then we're not living as Christ-ones. And they'll be the first to show us. The prophet will point out what is right and wrong, but the teacher will instruct us on how to know the difference. The evangelist will tell us how much Jesus loves us, but the teacher will tell us how to apply this love to our lives. The pastor will inform us as to areas of our life that need healing and deliverance and can guide us through it, but the teacher will teach us how to apply God's Word in our lives, so we walk out our healing. The teacher will give us step-by-step instruction, whereby we can pray for ourselves and teach others how to pray for themselves. The teacher empowers others how to use the Word as a weapon.

The downside of the teacher gift is that teachers can become counterfeit characters. They may perceive they are walking out the character of Christ, but they may be walking in pride or judgment of others. Seasoned teachers walk humbly before the Lord because they know the knowledge of the Word brings a greater responsibility. Teachers need to be challenged and not simply taken at their word.

Teachers need to be surrounded by pastors and prophets. The pastors work hand in hand with evangelists and teachers. The prophets bridge the apostles and the pastors. The evangelists need the assistance of the apostles and pastors. They all work together to form the body of Christ. They build bridges between the office of the gifts. They work to bring stability and reconciliation to the *ekklesia*. The *ekklesia* is the legislative body of Christ, the bride.

The Redemptive Gifts

We find the redemptive gifts in Romans 12: 6-8.

> *We have different gifts, according to the grace given to each of us. If your gift is prophesying, then prophesy in accordance with your faith; if it is serving, then serve; if it is teaching, then teach; if it is to encourage, then give encouragement; if it is giving, then give generously; if it is to lead, do it diligently; if it is to show mercy, do it cheerfully.*

Romans 12:6-8

Redemptive gifts are given to us when we are born. These are the gifts of God, just like the governmental gifts are from Jesus. We have a predisposition to a primary gift, but our environment can teach us to function in others to the point the primary gift is hard to identify. We are to exercise the use of all seven gifts just as Christ demonstrated. One of the easiest ways to identify your gift is to ask yourself, "What motivates you to do something the way you do it?"

Now, the redemptive gifts also come on the land. So, you can go into a territory and notice that your thought processing shifts a little bit.

For example, Tennessee is known for hospitality, especially toward strangers from all localities and walks of life. This is one reason it is popular with retirees throughout the nation. It is a welcoming place.

While we lived there, I acquired Tennessee's redemptive gift of hospitality, and it pulled something out of me that was new and fresh. In the past, if I would try to operate out of the hospitality gift on my own for too long, it felt more like an obligation which would exhaust me. But when I came to Tennessee, God's grace for hospitality took me beyond anything I could achieve on my own.

This is the nature of God. When we are weak, he is strong. He gives the Spirit of life that empowers us to do what we need to do at that moment. When we are in the right flow, ministry can be easy. Then, all of a sudden, we can be at our lowest and ready to just call it quits. But the Spirit will start moving and our spirits will revive, enabling us to finish what we need to minister.

Sometimes God will pair us with other people whose gifting complements ours. This is what the different gifts are all about. None of us has the strength in and of ourselves. We have some strength—we are created in God's image, after all—but we were never meant to go it alone.

When we combine our five governmental gifts with our seven redemptive gifts, we get 12 in all, right? They are designed to work together and overlap. The priestly role is fulfilled with the evangelist, pastor and teacher. The kingly role is the apostle and prophet. The reason the body of Christ has been more ineffective in kingship than effective is because many believe that the apostle and prophet no longer exist. (I don't believe in idol worship, but it exists.) The kingdom of God has not diminished. For instance, Jesus did not abolish the Law when he came, but he fulfilled it. Likewise, Jesus didn't abolish the roles of kings and priests, he fulfilled them. Then he even dared to tell us that greater things than he did we shall do. How can we do that when we deny our authority, or we say we can only hear God through the Word? You hear God's voice like your conscious voice, the same one that tells you, *You really shouldn't do that,* or *You'd better take care of that.* If we can hear the voice of God through our consciousness, then all of the other gifts exist. You are a king and priest.

Your livelihood grows as you train yourself to hear God in all areas of your life and act upon his commands. He will bless you abundantly more than you can ever ask for or imagine. He desires good things for you. The priests were provided for through the other tribes while they made the atonement necessary for others to stay in good standing with God. The king was also, but he used his blessings to expand the territory, build an army for defense and gain in riches while he ruled in his territory. Now through Jesus Christ, we are able to make atonement for ourselves through the blood of Jesus by repenting and asking him to forgive us. In addition, we can build and strategize for the growth of God's kingdom. He will bestow upon us the abundance of his kingdom

MESSIANIC

IDENTITY

9

MESSIANIC TEACHING

The term "messianic" refers to the Messiah, who is Jesus Christ. In many circles, people think that "messianic" is a term related to the Jewish people. Yes, Jesus came first for the Jews. He came to fulfill the prophesied Word of God, and so, he came to God's people. But as the Jews rejected him, his gospel expanded to the rest of the world.

> *He was in the world, and though the world was made through him, the world did not recognize him. He came to that which was his own, but his own did not receive him. Yet to all who did receive him, to those who believed in his name, he gave the right to become children of God—children born not of natural descent, nor of human decision or a husband's will, but born of God.*

> John 1:10-13

This fact, that the Gentiles were co-heirs with the Jews, was delivered in dramatic fashion when Peter, a devout Jew prior to Jesus, was sent to the house of Cornelius. In sending him on his way, God spoke clearly to Peter about changing his attitude toward the Gentiles.

> *About noon the following day as they were on their journey and approaching the city, Peter went up on the roof to pray. He became hungry and wanted something to eat, and while the meal was being prepared, he fell into a trance. He saw heaven opened and something like a large sheet being let down to earth by its four corners. It contained all kinds of four-footed animals, as well as reptiles and birds. Then a voice told him, "Get up, Peter. Kill and eat."*

"Surely not, Lord!" Peter replied. "I have never eaten anything impure or unclean."

The voice spoke to him a second time, "Do not call anything impure that God has made clean."

Acts 10:9-15

Philip also bore this message. He was sent to an Ethiopian eunuch who was reading the book of Isaiah. Phillip illuminated it for him, explaining the good news about Jesus and even baptizing the man. Then he was translated from there into the land where he supposed to be, where revival was breaking out.

Both of these were messianic encounters. The term *messianic* simply means you believe the Messiah to be Jesus Christ, the prophesied Savior who walked the earth. He was more than a prophet, more than a teacher, more than an evangelist. He was the living, breathing Messiah. In Hebrew, the original form is *Mashiyach*, reference number is 4898, which means *anointed*; of the Messiah, Messianic prince; of the king of Israel; of the high priest of Israel; of Cyrus; and of the patriarchs as anointed kings. That's what *messianic* means. The true form of believer is messianic.

In the concordance, the word *messiah* in Greek is *Messias*, reference number 3322, meaning *anointed*; the *Greek* form of Messiah; *a name of Christ*. Please note that the definition gives a reference back to the Greek meaning and adds as a second definition: "a name of Christ." There are only two scriptures where the word *Christian* is used. The first time is John 1:41. There is a phrase that states, "Messiah (which translated means Christ)." This tells me a translator has made a definition of the word *Christ* since the word *messiah* is the root of Christ and not the other way around. However, if Christ is defined as Jesus and Jesus is recognized as the Messiah, we are all messianic Christians. So then, when you accept Jesus as your personal Lord and Savior, repent of your sins, and he forgives you; you are saved. Therefore, you begin to take on the character of Jesus.

Identity of Christ

To the Jews in the days of the early church, there were two classes of people: pagans and Jews. Further, there was one place for the Jews to gather and worship. That was the temple. You either believed and worshipped God in the temple, or you worshipped idols as the pagans did. Some Jews corrupted their belief system by doing both, hedging their bets against the unseen day of judgment.

Yet, God's intent for purity was clear. In the Old Testament, the Lord's message to his chosen people, the Jews, was consistent: *Put away your idols, I'm all you need.* Then Jesus the Messiah came to earth with the same message: *Put away your idols. I'm here and I'm all you need. I'm born to pay the price. I will be crucified and resurrected for your redemption.* Of course, the Jews didn't listen to Jesus any better than they listened to the Father, and so a power struggle ensued in both the natural and the spiritual.

A New Temple

As this epic clash played out, the place of worship for the Jewish community remained the temple. Jesus followed this tradition. As a boy, where did Jesus hang out? Do you remember reading about when he disappeared for three days at age 12? He went into the temple and taught with knowledge far beyond the average twelve-year-old of his day. It confounded the wise and amazed the simple in attendance. Later, after his baptism by John, Jesus entered the temple to teach, challenging the corrupted precepts upon which the present temple worship and customs were based. Although most of the leaders rejected him, the people gathered around him to hear his words. Some believed and began following him, risking expulsion from the temple, and being ostracized from society. But others rejected him just as they rejected his Father, choosing instead to remain securely ensconced in temple life.

It would not remain secure for long, however. Conflict raged within the Jewish temple; everything was thrown into upheaval by Jesus' presence. The priest and the kings debated furiously among themselves: *What do we do with this Messiah? What do we do with this man who calls himself the Christ?*

And what do we do about all these people who now believe in him? They can't come into the temple any longer, it would be blasphemy. They know the rituals, they've studied the prophets, and they know the laws of Moses. This is the lifestyle they've lived but they believe this Jesus is the Messiah. Where do they go? They can't come here.

And so, the early believers in Christ were excluded from the temple. Because the temple was the center of Jewish life, it was like being displaced from your home. It is the same today. Anyone who has walked in Christ for long has experienced some sense of being displaced from a spiritual home before, especially if you're forward-thinking.

These are the new things that God's doing!

No, they're not. God's doing what he has always done. And he only uses us!

Yes, they are! He is doing something new! He really is!

It can't be. God would have sent the message through us, not you!

Well, maybe he did, and you missed it?

Get out!

Jesus put it this way:

> This is why I speak to them in parables: Though seeing, they do not see; though hearing, they do not hear or understand. In them is fulfilled the prophecy of Isaiah:
>
> "'You will be ever hearing but never understanding;
>
> you will be ever seeing but never perceiving.
>
> For this people's heart has become calloused;
>
> they hardly hear with their ears,
>
> and they have closed their eyes.
>
> Otherwise they might see with their eyes,
>
> hear with their ears,

understand with their hearts

and turn, and I would heal them."

Matthew 13:13-15

It happened when Jesus walked the earth, and it's happening today. We might even see a time in our churches when what we are operating in is so forward that the church itself doesn't even know what to do with us. We don't fit with them, but we don't fit without them either.

What shall we do?

We will carry the identity of Christ with us. Our identity is forged in him. The Name of God is on our foreheads and has marked us for eternity. His Spirit resides within us. It's there! It's part of us now, but we have to recognize it. We have to know our identity in Christ, and we have to find a way to continue on behalf of his kingdom, even if we're expelled from certain circles. We continue to walk in his love and his purposes and never take our eyes off of him.

Don't forget: We are never alone.

Keep your lives free from the love of money and be content with what you have, because God has said, "Never will I leave you; never will I forsake you."

So we say with confidence, "The Lord is my helper; I will not be afraid. What can mere mortals do to me?"

Hebrews 13:5-6

But the Advocate, the Holy Spirit, whom the Father will send in my name, will teach you all things and will remind you of everything I have said to you. Peace I leave with you; my peace I give you. I do not give to you as the world gives. Do not let your hearts be troubled and do not be afraid.

John 14:26-27

Then Jesus came to them and said, "All authority in heaven and on earth has been given to me. Therefore go and make disciples of all nations, baptizing them in the name of the Father and of the Son and of the Holy Spirit, and teaching them to obey everything I have commanded you. And surely I am with you always, to the very end of the age."

Matthew 28:18-20

When persecution began, the disciples fled to different cities. The good news is that revival broke out wherever they went. The people now excluded from the temple needed somewhere to meet, and in some instances, places to hide from persecution. Hence, they established home churches. Now, instead of one temple, there were many temples. Instead of one priest, all believers were of a royal priesthood.

But you are a chosen people, a royal priesthood, a holy nation, God's special possession, that you may declare the praises of him who called you out of darkness into his wonderful light.

1 Peter 2:9

This shift from two separate belief systems (Judaism and Paganism) to three (Christianity) shook the foundation of the earth. Every nation felt the change brought about by one man—the Son of God—who some refused to acknowledge and others gave their lives to follow. The chief priests did not want to acknowledge him as the King of Kings, but he transformed the world anyway. That was the first great awakening. It continued despite many of the apostles being killed. It flourished under the most difficult circumstances. And we're still here today. The life of God that builds momentum and continues to move forward doesn't digress. Life is progress. God's Kingdom will rule the earth. It's only a matter of time.

When Jesus came on the scene, John the Baptist had laid that foundation for Him. So, who are the "John the Baptists" in your midst today? Can you identify them? They are the ones declaring: "This is the day of the Lord! He is here in our midst. He is coming. Watch and behold, you will see the Messiah."

It could be you. You may be the one who is supposed to start declaring the way of the Lord.

Identity In Christ

Our identity is in Christ. This makes us messianic believers. Why is this so important? Because the enemy is doing everything he can to destroy the integrity of Christianity by assaulting what it even means to be a Christian—our identity.

The tools of his trade include the people who call themselves Christians but in truth, bear little resemblance to Christ. Certainly, none of us are perfect. We are all on a journey. But it is a journey from the inside out: "Christ in you, the hope of glory" (Colossians 1:27). We are the out-raying of the Divine (see Hebrews 1:3). Our lives bear the imprint of Almighty God who bestowed his Spirit within us, the same power that erupted at creation and caused worlds to appear out of the void; the same Spirit that fell on Pentecost and revealed to all the Word of God.

Fake Christianity knows little of this reality, and so it is fodder for the enemy's schemes. Cults that kill thousands and purport to be Christian convince the world that we are a violent religion at worst, or an inert belief system at best. Anything to take away from the impact that the Lord desires to have on a world that so desperately needs him. The Kingdom of God is coming to the earth, more so every day. The battle is for the hearts and minds of the people, some who stand without, debating whether to join or not, and some who are within, wondering if it's all worth it, if their faith can hold and grow, if any of this can help real-world problems.

> *Dear children, let us not love with words or speech but with actions and in truth.*
>
> 1 John 3:18

Really, both sides have a point. Words are empty unless they have action behind them. I can say I'm going to make a quilt, but if I don't gather the fabric, purchase the thread, cut out the pieces, plan my design...in short, if I don't put the resources together and set aside the time to actually put my hand to it, guess what? I'm not making a quilt. I'm only fantasizing.

God is weaving the final tapestry of the day. We are part of it. But we have to be able to demonstrate the character and love of Christ. We have to be able to look at the New Testament and see it within us. We have to be able to compare Matthew, Mark, Luke, and John, to see what Jesus did to demonstrate character and love. He also commissioned the disciples to do the same. It's not enough to *join* him; you must *become* like him. It's called identity.

When Jesus left the disciples and returned to the Father, it was left to his disciples to further the work. Christ was no longer there, but the Holy Spirit was. And when the Apostles died, others took over from them. Our role is to pick up where the previous generation left off. Attending church is good, but our identity is not in church. Our identity is in Christ, and it is to become everything that we do. I don't stop being Rebecca just because I go home. I don't stop being Crispin's wife just because he goes out of town. These are components of my identity, and they are integral to who I am, regardless of circumstance

So it is with Christ. Our identity as Christ-ones is not something we put on. It's not a matter of learning Bible verses and spouting off the right things to say, buying different clothes or even dressing a certain way. Identity is not conformity in a superficial sense. It is the result of the ingrained presence of the eternal seed of God coming to fruition.

Birthright And Blessing

A birthright is received by passive action. We are born with it. It doesn't require any effort on our part. You might get a little bit of a headache, but other than that, there's nothing on your part that you have to do to activate the birthright. It's part of who you are.

Each of us has a unique birthright with certain characteristics and identifiers. My birthright from my parents bestows certain things. For one, it gives me my birth order. I'm the youngest of two; others are born the oldest or the middle children. We also inherit DNA, giving us red hair or blonde, gangly arms or stubby, a propensity for athletics or chess. Everything about us ties back to our parents who likely carry similar traits and passed them on to us.

Of course, no two children are alike, and experience counts as much as birthright. You can raise seven children in the same home and every one of their home experiences will be different. Why? Because of the varying personality dynamics of that home.

Similarly, when you come into Christ Jesus, you inherit your messianic identity. It's a spiritual birthright. You are of the kingdom of God, and the keys that Adam gave up have now been restored through Jesus' death on the cross and his resurrection. That is our messianic birthright that comes from being Christ-ones.

Now, we also inherit the birthright of Abraham, whether it's through adoption or actual Jewish blood. Either way, God says now we're all on an equal playing field. There's no one greater or lesser. This is the passive inheritance that comes by acknowledging Christ as a Lord and Savior. But we're not supposed to just stop with our inheritance and birthright. Yes, that's a blessing, but there's more.

Recall Jesus' parable of the prodigal son. He took his inheritance—a part of his birthright—and left for the world. But how much more could he have had if he would have stayed? The blessing of the inheritance would have continued to grow. That was his birthright. Unfortunately, he came to himself rather late: *I should've stayed with my father. I could be living so much better off if I had stayed. I'll go home and be a servant. Anything's better than this.*

We see the same attitude today with people who have tasted the goodness of the Lord, and yet, they just want that portion that makes them feel good at the time. They come into his presence, perhaps through a church or charity, get the goods to meet their immediate needs, and then they leave. This approach misses the true birthright. We are called to be doers of the Word.

In the Jewish community, the sons come into their inheritance at the age of thirteen. Why? So their fathers can help them steward what they have. *Hey dad, I've been thinking about this business transaction. What do you think? How do I approach that? Should I step away? What should I do?*

They now work together, man-to-man. Through the inheritance of the birthright, the son gradually takes control and begins to develop his portion. Not only does he have the birthright, but he's also complementing the birthright by putting his hands into it to see it grow.

That's what God wants us to do. We have to put our hands to our birthright to watch it grow and develop. One way we do this is by expanding the knowledge of those around us. If we don't demonstrate Christ in us, how are others supposed to know what Christ looks like? How well do we represent him?

Developing the seed requires action. It starts as a passive transaction. That is the nature of salvation. We receive salvation by simply believing in Christ, recognizing that he has freed us from our sins, that we have been washed in the blood and our transgressions have been forgiven. It's a free gift. Jesus has already paid the price. But it doesn't remain so.

As we continue to put the seed forward—if we're really seeking the Lord and we understand our identity in Him—we begin to put our hands to that seed from the redemptive side. This is how we operate in a blessing. It is the multiplication factor of momentum.

Yes, our parents leave a blessing for us to continue to grow, and part of that blessing comes from walking beside them. Similarly, by walking with the Lord, we received a blessing of things such as knowledge, wisdom, understanding, revelation, gifts, and talent. All of this comes just in learning the Lord and having Him active and ever-present in our lives.

And then the work begins.

Blessing Others

Just as our blessing is to come from the Father, it is also to go out from our lives to others. We bless people by loving them because love is seed. It has to grow because it's a part of God. The very nature of God is love. Everything that he does expands creation. The universe is ever expanding.

We, ourselves, are priests and kings. We help others come to Christ. We demonstrate that love of sacrifice. This is how the Kingdom of God grows.

The priests of the Old Testament went into the temple to sacrifice for the people and their sins. We follow the same spirit today, praying: *Lord, I want to help this community. Will you hear my cries? Will you minister to this community? Will you bless them through me? Will you multiply and expand their territory? Lord, will you begin to show up through healings in their bodies? Will you begin to give them wisdom? Will you begin to show them miracles, signs, and wonders?*

We bless them by forecasting their need and speaking it out in prayer. Prayer words are life. They activate a blessing in everything we put our mind to because as our mind thinks, our body follows, and so will everything else around us. We have dominion and we're taking authority. We are kings and we declare what happens on the earth.

You don't like something? Then change it. But change it through prayer first, through the release of blessing. Of course, you've got to see the need and recognize it before you can release anything prophetically. And yet, it doesn't stop there. Once released, you must respond to the Spirit's prompting. Be the arms and hands extended to meet the need.

> *If one of you says to them, "Go in peace; keep warm and well fed,"*
> *but does nothing about their physical needs, what good is it?*

> James 2:16

Redemptive Gifts

Freedom is knowing our identity in Christ. It's a free gift; it doesn't cost us anything; the price has already been paid. At salvation, our redemptive gifts are in us but they're amped up. We don't immediately recognize what they are, but after we come to Christ, they begin to grow within us.

The seven redemptive gifts are listed in Romans 12:6-8, as prophecy, serving, teaching, encouraging, giving, leading, and mercy. After salvation, our redemptive gifts come forward in our consciousness and we begin to activate them in the new life that comes through Jesus. It starts by seeing shifts in our personalities. *Wow, I don't remember thinking like that before. Where did that clarity come from?* Attitudes, approaches and paradigms begin to change. Our motivations are different. We begin to see things from God's perspective and sense his grace to impact the revealed areas of need.

Now, there's a difference between the desires of our natural personalities and our redemptive gifts. For instance, many people want to be prophet redemptive—one of the redemptive gifts. But if they really understood the gift, they would not want it. It requires a special grace. People confuse the real gift with what appears to be God's mandate to get in people's faces and tell them our version of the truth. Yes, every person, at some time in their life, wants to get in someone else's face. And the thought of doing that in God's Spirit seems juicy. But that is not how the prophetic works. In fact, that ardent desire to tell other people off is usually the indication of a need for personal growth. It highlights a lack of self-control and personal discipline. Just because you get in somebody's face and tell them like it is doesn't mean that you are prophet redemptive. It likely means you're judgmental and caustic.

The prophet redemptive gift begins and ends in the deepest prayer work imaginable. It takes effort to shift the spiritual forces that are obscuring people's lives with darkness. The part where the prophet actually gets to "tell somebody off" is the tip of the iceberg and, in fact, rarely happens. Most of the change is invisible to the natural eye.

As with all redemptive gifts, but more so the ones that share God's judgment with others, the same conviction that comes through a prophet is applied in far greater measure to the prophet's life. It is not an easy gift to have. Far from it.

Each of the redemptive gifts reveals the mind of Christ, shapes our lives, and motivates our conclusions. It drives how we respond to certain situations. Here's an example.

Imagine sitting around a table eating dinner and a server comes out with an overladen cart of desserts. There is a slight jiggle, and one dessert falls to the floor. The normally suave server is crestfallen.

Someone with a teaching gift says, "I knew that was going to happen. You could have seen it coming. There were too many desserts on that cart. You needed to make two trips."

Someone with an encouragement or mercy gift says, "It's OK, it wasn't your fault. Don't worry about it. It's OK. You're loved. We'll tip you extra."

Someone with the giver gift says, "Excuse me, can you bring another dessert? I'll pay for it."

Someone with the prophetic redemptive gift says, "Let's examine what could've done differently to prevent this from happening again" and then makes suggestions.

Now, in reading this example, you might be thinking: "Well, here's what I would think or do." This is important because whatever you are thinking right now reflects your own redemptive gift. The mind of Christ begins to operate through us as soon as we turn our hearts to him.

When we're filled with the spirit, there's something else that stirs within us to the core of our being. The redemptive gift is the mind of Christ. The way that we perceive a thing, the way we approach a thing, the way we move to action. All of this is through a redemptive gift, not a personality. There are personality traits in it, but remember, it's motivated through the mind of Christ in our spirit.

Governmental Gifts

The five governmental gifts are found in Ephesians 4:11-13. They are Apostle, prophet, evangelist, pastor, teacher.

When we receive the spirit, we are given our governmental gifts. They are like arms, designed to accomplish what has been engendered within us through our redemptive gifts. So, once we perceive a need through our redemptive gifts, our arms extend to build the bridge between what we desire and what eventually materializes.

Here's how this works.

The apostolic will see a need and issue direction. "This is where we need to go; this is what we need to do; we've got to go here and pray; we need to go there. We need to go to the hospital and visit them because they're there and I don't even think they have any family in town." The apostolic puts feet on the heart of God. They begin to move in the direction we need to go in. There's a need. We're going. Wherever the cloud of God is going, they are too. When the cloud stops, they stop and build. When the cloud moves again, they move.

The prophet will say, "Yes, I'm seeing that also and here's the Word of the Lord that backs that up." And they begin to release it through the Word and put life on it.

While the apostolic feet are moving forward and the prophetic voice is releasing it, the evangelist rouses everybody: "Do you all see this need? Did you all hear the prophet? Did you hear in which direction we're going? You all need to come because this is where we're going. If you don't go, you're going to miss it and you need to understand." So, they bring in the workers.

The pastor looks after everyone, ensuring they have the means to do what they're called to do. "You're going to need to get some gas before you go. You need to make sure that you've got some snacks because it's two hours there and back. Do you have money? Do you have a plan? A map? A compass? Did you take your anointing oil? Do you have tissues? Salt? Clean clothes?" They are making sure that the essentials are there.

The teacher provides all the reasons why they are doing what they are doing. "Well, the Word says that we anoint them. We lay hands on them. It says right here." The teacher provides the instruction to make sure we're all moving in the same direction as we hear God and follow his Spirit.

Manifestation Gifts

The nine manifestation gifts come from 1 Corinthians 12:7-11. They are word of wisdom, word of knowledge, faith, healing, miracles, prophecy, discerning of spirits, tongues, interpretation of tongues,

Now, you can operate in any of the gifts at any given point in time as you exercise your authority in Holy Spirit. There is one prerequisite: you must be willing. Just because you're a teacher-redemptive doesn't mean that you can't act as a server-redemptive all the time. We exercise all of these things. We grow. We can be apostolic and prophetic and teach all at the same time as the Spirit moves us. Indeed, the three categories of gifts are meant to flow together just as the Godhead of Father, Son and Spirit flow together.

Let's look at this on a practical level. Imagine you're in a place of business and you're speaking with someone. All of a sudden, you feel spiritual energy rise up within you.

You respond: "OK Holy Spirit. That's why I'm here. What will you have me do?"

Your spirit is alert and paying attention to what Holy Spirit has for you, showing you there's a purpose for you being here at this precise time. You have something to do. You're it. Your redemptive may look like a teacher or a pastor as you give them the truth of the Word that brings that person to repentance. It may look like putting an arm around someone and saying everything's going to be OK.

As you begin to motivate out of your governmental role, something's going to happen. Through obedience, you receive a manifestation gift: a word of wisdom, a word of knowledge or faith.

"I'm believing for you; I believe that this isn't over. God wants to minister to you through this. Can I pray with you?"

Miracles, prophecy, and discerning of spirits begin to operate.

"I'm sensing that there's a spirit of depression around you. Can I pray with you and break that off? Can we just pray and agree right now that that thing is not going to be victorious in your life?"

Speaking in tongues and interpretation are activated as you pray. The person responds as you speak their heart in prayer, things they have told no one, secrets only God knows.

Finally, you are able to remove the stronghold and speak quiet words of instruction into their newly opened heart. Yes, the motivation is prophetic: *Never let this happen again.* But the means to accomplish it may be teaching: *Here's how you got into that mess. Here's how to avoid it in the future.* It may be couched in mercy: *There is no condemnation, so don't slip into it.* And finally, you send them on their way with an apostolic mandate: *Go and sin no more.*

Ministering to people takes our redemptive gifts, our governmental gifts and our manifestation gifts working together. Just as the Godhead works together as three are one, we can't differentiate one from the other. Yes, they are obviously separate, but each one is nothing without the others. The parts are nothing without the whole.

The end product looks like the fruits of the Spirit: love, joy, peace, patience, kindness, goodness, faithfulness, gentleness, self-control (Galatians 5). Undergirding all of this is love. It's hard to minister to a person if you're not activated in love. Through love, you feel the character of God within you, and it produces fruit. It could be a ministry of peace if someone is going through anguish or distress. Or you might be the very presence that they need to bring things back into proper alignment, saving them from going out and desperately doing something tragic or self-destructive.

There is no need to fear any of these gifts. They are from God. The gifts are used to restore our relationship to the fulness of God. Adam and Eve had no barriers between them and God. God walked with them in the cool of the evening. They conversed easily. God uses these gifts to remove the barriers between us and him. He longs for us to commune with him night and day. When we commune with God, we know his heart. When he is cut off from others, he will use us as a conduit for his love. This way, he encourages others and shares glimpses of himself, so they might enter into his loving-kindness. Our gifts are to be used to build one another up and not used to tear each other down. He made us the way he intended, for his purposes. We need to exercise our gifts and operate in them in purity and righteousness.

Identity

As Christ-ones, our identity is in Christ and should be reflected in everything we do. It is not something that we turn on and turn off. It's a vital part of us. If I look in the mirror, I should see the representation of Christ. I have to be able to recognize myself through the fruits of the Spirit, the governmental gifts, the manifestation gifts, and the redemptive gifts. I have to see that part of me that has been restored through my innermost being because the rest of me will pass away someday. But the things that are within are eternal. Those things will last because they have the breath of God on them.

We have to understand who we are. We represent a reflection of the Lord. Our identity is tied up in our relationship with him. Our blood and spirits have mingled with our Creator, and a process is underway to manifest his presence on earth. We may not fully look like the best butterfly yet. We might still be in a cocoon process. Yes, we might have to go back to a cocoon process a couple of different times. (I know I do all the time.) But we're working together to manifest the Kingdom of God through our new identity.

As a mature Christ-one—tested, tried, and grown—I can no longer see a separation of where Christ in me ends or begins. I remember one time being so desperate to see God's hand move in a situation that I was trying to barter with him in the midst of my grief, standing outside my back patio, saying, "God, I'm just ready to walk away from you. I cannot do this anymore. It just hurts so much." And I just wept.

Finally, I reached an inexorable conclusion: "Lord, the thing is, I can't walk away from you because I no longer know who I am without you."

I didn't really understand my words at that time, but I knew I was too far into my faith in him to give up. I couldn't turn back now. And today, I'm glad I didn't turn back. It was all part of the process, one that still reveals remnants of doubt and unbelief in myself. It grieves me. I don't want this lack of faith in me. I only want to see the fullness of Christ. And I know that he is faithful to bring it to be.

Therein lies our identity. He is who he says he is. He does what he says he'll do. He is not a man that he should lie. We should all be able to stand in faith, unwavering in our identity in him. That is our quest.

10

SOUND IDENTITY

In the beginning God created the heavens and the earth. Now the earth was formless and empty, darkness was over the surface of the deep, and the Spirit of God was hovering over the waters. And God said, "Let there be light," and there was light.

Genesis 1:1-3

God created the world with his sound. He commanded light to come into existence—the literal interpretation of his words has been rendered by some as: "'Light, BE!' And light was." Time began from that moment, arising from the sound that was the essence of the Creator.

The qualities of light and sound remain constant throughout the universe. There is a direct correlation between light, color, sound, and velocity.

Just as the light of Jesus shines through us and draws all men to us, so does the sound that we release. In our sound is the power of life and death. The sound of righteousness draws people. Think about what happened on the day of Pentecost:

Now there were staying in Jerusalem God-fearing Jews from every nation under heaven. When they heard this sound, a crowd came together in bewilderment, because each one heard their own language being spoken.

Acts 2:5-6

When the people from every nation heard the sound of the Spirit emanating from the upper room, they were bewildered, but they were also drawn to it. This culminated in the first, great evangelistic outreach of the new church. Peter declared that the sound was not from drunkards, but that which was promised in Joel: "I will pour out my Spirit in those days" (Acts 2:18). The sound they heard was spirit—*the* Spirit—the essence of the Creator. And a new work had begun as thousands received Jesus that day.

The sound of our praise and worship draws the Father's presence in an intimate way.

Sound is defined as:

1. the sensation produced by stimulation of the organs of hearing by vibrations transmitted through the air or other medium
2. mechanical vibrations traveling through air
3. a noise, vocal utterance, musical tone, or the like
4. a distinctive, characteristic, or recognizable musical style
5. phonetics or speech sound
6. to make or emit a call or summons; to be heard, or convey a certain message

This is what Moses heard when he encountered God on the mountain.

> *On the morning of the third day there was thunder and lightning, with a thick cloud over the mountain, and a very loud trumpet blast. Everyone in the camp trembled. Then Moses led the people out of the camp to meet with God, and they stood at the foot of the mountain. Mount Sinai was covered with smoke, because the Lord descended on it in fire. The smoke billowed up from it like smoke from a furnace, and the whole mountain trembled violently. As the sound of the trumpet grew louder and louder, Moses spoke and the voice of God answered him.*

> Exodus 19:16-19

God spoke to Moses at Mount Sinai. There was the sound of a trumpet blast, with thunder and lightning, but a cloud of smoke enveloped it and the mountain trembled. The *mountain* trembled! That was its sound in response to the sound of its Creator.

Sound has other definitions as well:

1. free from injury, damage, defect, disease
2. financially strong, secure, or reliable
3. competent, sensible, or valid, having no defect as to truth, justice, wisdom, or reason
4. of substantial or enduring character
5. vigorous, thorough, or severe
6. free from moral defect or weakness, upright, honest or good, honorable or loyal

Our God is sound in all his ways: wisdom, knowledge, understanding, righteous judgment and truth. God's ways are not our ways. They are higher. Likewise, Titus 2 tells us to "teach what is appropriate to sound doctrine" (Titus 2:1).

Finally, sound can be defined as a verb tense used with an object such as to measure or try the depth of water or hole by letting down a lead or plummet at the end of a line.

The Father will test our depth by bringing up bits of matter from the depths of our beings for cleansing. When gold ore is put to the fire, the impurities will surface, leaving behind pure gold. This is what God does to us. He purifies us through the heat of trials, tests and tribulations. His goal is to make us the purest gold and in so doing, secure the soundness of our identity. "Deep calls to deep" (Psalm 42:7). If we are going to go deeper with God, we have to be willing to go deeper into our identity to extract the impurities that do not belong there.

As God spoke on day one of this world, his sound created such a vibration that it caused a world of change. His sound is not merely noise. It is the soundness of sound expressing the purity of holiness.

Sound and Light

Through his sound, God created light. We can reason, then, that both sound and light were present together on the first day, and therefore, when we have his sound, we have his light.

Scientifically speaking, light and sound are the results of waves—energy waves (light) and molecular waves (sound). Further, certain colors and sounds can be associated with each other.

White light is not really a color. It is the combination of every color of the visible light spectrum. This is why sunlight shined through a prism will emerge as an array of colors: red, orange, yellow, green, blue, indigo, violet—the rainbow colors. These colors represent the varying contributing wavelengths of light that comprise white light.

As strange as it may seem, sound has the ability to bend light, thus altering its frequency. From this fact, it can be reasoned that sound can change the color of light. This is because bending light alters its wavelength, and the color of light is determined by its wavelength.

Our Sounds on The Land

Synesthesia is described as a sensation in which a sensory or cognitive pathway leads to automatic, involuntary experiences in a second sensory or cognitive pathway. An example of this is when a person sees colors of crimson when they hear a trumpet played. However, another may see colors of the rainbow when a musical scale is played on a piano. Therefore, let us conclude that sound and light interact with one another to produce colors: both seen and unseen.

According to Dr. Masaru Emoto, when water was used in his experiments, it represented a "reflection of our reality," in that positive energies and vibrations could change the physical structure of water. He tested theories in which he spoke or played negatively charged sounds into water, snowflakes and rice, and then tested the same theory using positive words or sounds. While most people accept that sound has the ability to change our emotional state of being, Emoto argues that it can actually change our physical state on a molecular level. It changes who we are.

Sound creates vibration, and vibration affects our beings. Some people use crystals to enhance their moods, basing the practice on the vibrations emitted by the crystals. People can also feel vibrations from trees and soil—

the land. Vibration is one of the ways that people respond to each other and to their environment.

Note: We *must* be careful how we use such things, because the land will vomit us out if we are found guilty of the detestable things according to Deuteronomy 18 and Leviticus 18. These scriptures verify that the land echoes what we release in it, thus affecting what we receive from it.

The nation of Israel is such a historic ancient place that the very vibrations of the land are contagious to one's physical body. The sound that is in the land will resonate within you.

Vibrations are a part of our identity. Consider the light that we emit from our eyes. This is part of our subconscious identity. Also, the vibrations from speaking the letters of the Hebraic alphabet cause shapes to form.

(Examples of this phenomenon are available via the internet, as are NASA recordings of the sounds of earth and other celestial bodies.)

Power of A Name

The speaking of a name is powerful. For example, if my mother softly says my name as I am relaxing, I will remain in a restful state. However, if she calls me by my full name, I will jerk to attention in maximum alertness (and perhaps a little fear).

The sound of your name can cause a reaction within you and others. This is because your name causes a vibration in the atmosphere and the land around you. As with many things related to metaphysics, we have terms for the experience, even if we lack adequate definitions. We usually refer to the negative response of this interaction as a stirring in the pit of our stomachs, or perhaps a flutter if it is a positive reaction. Again, consider the two different reactions I have to my mother speaking my name: one of comfort and one of alarm, depending on her tone, which is a variation in vibration.

I considered all of this when it came time to name each of my children. I researched the origin and meanings of potential names. For example, if I say: "Nike," what does your mind think? Shoes? Or their slogan: *Just do it*?

You see, the shoe brand helps you identify with a few thoughts by simply using a single word name: Nike.

Several years ago, I used to just say, "Nike" when I wanted something done. I understood the context of the name as: *Just do it*. But soon thereafter, I became convicted about this. So, I asked the Lord why this was. Copyright infringement? No. He told me to look up the meaning of the phrase's origins. Although I understood the connotation for the name in relation to its marketing, I was missing a key component. It turns out that *Nike* is known in ancient Greek religion as the goddess of victory from the city of Ephesus.

Now, does this mean that the Nike company dedicates itself to this Greek goddess? I doubt it. Further, I am in no way inferring this. However, some qualities go beyond immediate intent. Because of this, it behooves us to question what brands we are drawn to and what certain names really mean in the spirit. Maybe some reflect something about us regarding our generational line or deeper things within us.

In my case, I repented for replacing the statement, "Just do it," with the name *Nike*. This was my personal conviction, however. This is not a doctrine. (Don't go burning your running shoes, OK?)

The lesson here is that your name means something. It is a part of your identity. It is as much a part of you as your DNA. And associations often go unnoticed.

It has also been proven that your DNA provides a genetic song. There are only so many protein combinations that make up your DNA code that can be formatted into the sequencing of musical notes which will create your personal DNA song. Therefore, if your very DNA has the ability to reflect musical qualities, then does it make a subconscious detectable sound? Well, if you gently place your fingers over both of your ears, you can hear the roaring sound of your blood flowing through your veins. That causes a vibration, and vibrations make up sound. Is that what God meant when he said that Able's blood called out from the ground? Was it still vibrating? Further, does the land in Israel vibrate because Jesus' blood calls out from the ground there?

Jesus was the only human to walk this earth with the DNA of God. When you repent of your sins and accept Jesus as your personal Savior, you are made new through the shedding of his blood. The sound constantly playing within you becomes a reflection of his DNA in you. You now have a redeemed *sound* identity. Your sound resonates through your generational line and creates a newer more vibrant sound. In the spirit realm, it is as unmistakable as your luminous light. Father knows you by your spirit, consisting of light and sound.

The Israelites had a sound. When Moses was moving the people out of the wilderness, the Lord clearly defined the boundaries of the Promised Land. Twelve spies went into the land. Ten returned with daunting reports of fearful threats, but two—Joshua and Caleb—came back with a different report. *Yes, there are hard obstacles, but we can take them.* Because the prevailing doubt of the 10 spies affected the people, the Lord waited to move Israel into the Promised Land. His approach was: *We're going to let those doubters and naysayers stay right here. I have all the time in the world. We can do this forever if you want. But I've got a land for you, and I'm going to put you in that land when you are ready.*

God delayed Israel's entrance to the Promised Land for an entire generation so that the language of doubt and unbelief would be left in the wilderness. He does the same today. He does not want our doubt and unbelief to come with us into his promise for us. The promise is our legacy. It is our inheritance. Therefore, we have to abandon our doubt and unbelief. If we cannot overcome our unbelieving language, we perish in the wilderness like the doubting generation of Israel. Even though we stand at the threshold with the Promised Land within sight, we will remain that one faith-step away from our Promised Land, suspended from the progression of our inherited destiny until our faith catches up to God's purpose.

Joshua and Caleb took a different approach from the doubters. Their words held power: *Hey, we can go in there. We can fight. We can do it.* And they were the ones who eventually led the next generation of Israel into the

Promised Land. Their sound released them in the destiny God had for them. Otherwise, they would have perished in the desert with their doubting generation.

Our Prophetic Sound

We have to release the prophetic sound over the land as our possession, just as God spoke it first, a type and shadow of things to come.

In the beginning, God speaks our promises and we walk them out in faith. We receive by going through the motions, doing what we're supposed to do. Then, when we gain some maturity, the Lord puts us right where we're supposed to be and conveys the message of maturity: *OK, this next part is yours. You've got to take responsibility for this. I've done all I can do. Until you take that step of faith, you won't have this.*

Now it's on us. Now we have to exercise our faith to receive the promise. The land is the promise of our inheritance, but the promise is fulfilled through our spoken word. Before we can occupy the land, we first have to see it. The next vital step in receiving the promise is for us to declare that it is ours.

God will bless our lives, but we have to do our part. He will give us a better job, but we have to go out and search for it. He will present financial opportunities, but we have to adjust our spending, learn to budget better, manage risk, and perhaps acquire some discipline. Maybe we want to upsize, but we really need to downsize. Other times, we might want to downsize but he upsizes us. The key is knowing what God wants for us at any given time. To come into the promise, we have to be in God's timing, not ours.

Our words can cancel an assignment. The promise can be laid out right in front of us, but by the negative testimony of our words, we can wander in the wilderness and die there. That is, unless we turn around and say, "God I repent. I released the wrong sound over the land. The land is your inheritance."

Notice what we do: *Say...*

God's Sound

There's a sound that is God's sound. When He speaks, we recognize his language. Is God's language English? No, English is one of the newest languages around. God's language is Hebrew. The beautiful thing about Hebrew is that it not only demonstrates a fluidity of sounds released in unison with Abba Father, but it also creates a picture. It's a symbol of God's identity, a symbol of his promise to us, and it is to all things life-giving.

Every letter in Hebrew is connected to God, which is the very sound of life. When He spoke, there *was*. As he speaks, there *is* and *remains*. It becomes an eternal component to life in God's language.

I'm not a Hebrew scholar, but when God gives me a word or scripture, I go back and study what he's saying in the depths of himself. That is his language. When I'm reading scripture, there are times when it will mean one thing, but when I come back through a different situation and read that scripture again, it means something more as well.

God's Word is alive. It is a living Word. It constantly changes, as does any living thing. Because I am living, I am growing. I don't look six years old anymore. As I am in God's Spirit, I am constantly changing—body, soul, and spirit. As part of that growth, the language of my spirit is becoming more and more of God's language and less of my own.

11

WORD

There is a time for everything, and a season for
every activity

under the heavens...

a time to tear and a time to mend,

a time to be silent and a time to speak,

a time to love and a time to hate,

a time for war and a time for peace.

Ecclesiastes 3:1, 7-8

Walking out our identity involves different times and seasons. What worked in one place will not work in another. Our prayer life, our access to the Spirit, our relationships with others and the challenges that come with them, will vary accordingly. We must learn to recognize the season we are in—when it's time to work and when it's time to rest. We are in a new season right now. The fact that you are reading this and partaking of the teaching means you sense it as well. There are unseen events transpiring in the spirit realm. God is moving and so must we.

In previous lessons, we've looked at the messianic. We've also looked at our redemptive gifts, our sound, our historical markers, and our physical markers. And yet, it all comes down to God's Word. We cannot overlook the sound of his Word. Be it written, heard, sensed, condensed, debated, mulled over, embraced or ignored throughout time, it's still the Word, as true today as it was for thousands of years. Even before we had a book or scrolls or clay tablets or even verbal records, we had the Word from God to our spirits. Historically, the sound of the Word was released regularly among God's people so that nothing was left out, nothing was void in the lives of God's people. The children of Jewish families knew the Word as part of their upbringing. It was studied, memorized, and used as a part of their everyday lives. When God spoke, he uttered his Word as life and creation all at once. Breath came from him and created what was in his heart.

As the rain and the snow

come down from heaven,

and do not return to it

without watering the earth

and making it bud and flourish,

so that it yields seed for the sower and bread for the eater,

so is my word that goes out from my mouth:

It will not return to me empty,

but will accomplish what I desire

and achieve the purpose for which I sent it.

Isaiah 55:10-11

We still have his living Word today. Whether it is on a page, etched on parchment, or spoken, it is still his Word. As believers, his Word now lives within us. It is alive. It is well. It has spirit all through it. Before the foundations of the world, there was God's Word.

When we release his Word into the earth, we marry the sound that has been placed within us through this thing that we call a physical body. That sound resonates through our blood and our DNA. It is in everything that we do. It is a sound that marries with the sound of his eternal Word—a sound that has no beginning, no end, but yet the beginning and end are found within it.

As we release our sound in the earth, we become the salt of the earth, and then the earth yields what it's supposed to yield as our provision. God created the earth for our purposes. It starts with sound. We have our sound; God has his sound. His was first. It was in the beginning while the earth was void. When there was nothing else, there was the sound of God, and the sound was the Word.

> *In the beginning was the Word, and the Word was with God, and*
> *the Word was God.*

John 1:1

The Word was God. When Jesus came, he came as the living Word. He came to distribute the Word, to fulfill it and re-establish it among men. Although we think of the Trinity as the Father, Son and Holy Spirit, there remains one vital component: The Word. It is the Word that makes them all one. The Word is God's life, his very breath. The Word is our all in all.

> *In the beginning God created the heavens and the earth. Now the*
> *earth was formless and empty, darkness was over the surface of*
> *the deep, and the Spirit of God was hovering over the waters. And*
> *God said...*

Genesis 1:1-3

There's more of God's Word than his written Word. What we have come to know through the Bible has been cut down and transcribed into different languages, and because of this, we've lost some revelation and understanding. Yet what remains is still the Word. It is the Word we've come to know, but there are more Words. Before time began, there was God's Word. It precedes everything else. It is eternal, with no beginning or end. God's Word is sound, creativity and life. Everything around us came from words.

Remember:

> *The tongue has the power of life and death, and those who love it*
> *will eat its fruit.*

Proverbs 18:21

Although there is more to God's Word than what is written in the Bible, we cannot divert from what is recorded there. God gave us his written Word to test other words brought forth in the Spirit. This is vital to our integrity. Every prophetic word needs to align with the written Word. This is one reason God gave us teachers.

Teachers help us understand the written Word. Of course, it's up to us to search a thing out, but we have the giftings of those around us to keep us safely ensconced in God's protective will. There are many false words out there, and no end to deception. This is why we are to live and breathe the Word—God's Word. As I said in previous chapters, I don't even like to pray in my own language anymore because I might not say what the Father's heart is. When I pray in his language, however, everything that he wants to release on this earth is dispatched because the language of God is understood on the earth.

The earth understands the sound that we release. It knows when we testify for the Word of God, and when we testify against it. It blesses the earth when we speak God's Word, and it injures the earth when we speak against the truth of God and his Word. It shakes the very foundation on which we stand when we utter words that do not come out of his testimony. "For in him we live and move and have our being" (Acts 17:28). He is the Word.

When you feed yourself with the Word, meditating night and day, feeding your heart with the Word, you are acquiring the Word that is to be released through you. You become the living and breathing testimony of God's Word. It becomes alive in you.

The Word is to become part of our identities. He made that abundantly clear. As he spoke, the Word was released from him into us, his people.

> *Let the message of Christ dwell among you richly as you teach*
> *and admonish one another with all wisdom through psalms,*
> *hymns, and songs from the Spirit, singing to God with gratitude*
> *in your hearts.*

Colossians 3:16

As we release our sound through hymns and spiritual songs, we marry the very notes of our love and devotion to the Father, Son and Spirit. It marries with the Word and becomes an edification, a sacrifice, incense to the Lord that he finds as a sweet aroma that draws his presence to us. He abides with us, and it brings him back into the garden, back to that glorious place where we are filled with his glory and established as sons and daughters of God standing beside Christ. With him, our identity is fully released. Further, our flesh is hidden by the glory as we step behind the sound of the Word being released.

My Lesson

Years ago, I struggled with some things that God was leading me into. It came down to this: "Lord, your Word has lost its savor to me." I had been through some tough times and felt like a tumbleweed blown around and stuck until the wind catches it and it rolls away again. "God, your Word has become bitter to my taste because I know what your Word says. I have it in my heart. I have stood on it through thick and thin. I have used it as my defense even when I didn't need a defense. I have stood and believed because your promises are yes and amen. They are forever. They have no end. Lord, I have stood on your Word. I have declared your Word. I have released your Word. I have stewarded your Word. And yet, it has become bitter to me. Too much disappointment, disillusionment, strife, confusion, anger, rage, hatred, deception, rejection, and gossip. Did I leave anything out, Lord? Just fill it in."

As these dark forces were raging through me, the Father said, "I'm going to put you on a fast. When you read my Word daily, you're going to subsist on that Word."

Well, I knew this was exactly what I needed to do by the fact that it was difficult for me at first. But it got easier as the days went by. When I would open my mouth to talk to someone, I would begin to prophesy, and the Word would come forth out of me. I felt healing in my heart as the Word went in and came back out in power. I was being restored.

It came to a point where I looked forward to reading the Word because I understood that I was becoming one with it again. I had rediscovered that place of intimacy where the Word was sweet to me. And God said: "You've been communing with me every day. As you eat my Word, you are eating my flesh. You are partaking of me." I came from that place ready to move on. It didn't mean that the struggle around me changed. It was still there. But how I interacted with it did change, because the position that I came from now was that place of intimacy with the Word. It became my sound. It became my identity again. When everything around me was trying to diminish and destroy my identity to where I didn't know where I was coming from or going to, I finally had a point of reference—the Word.

Release the Word

We have to know how to release the Word. It is our sound. It is that thing that trumps everything. The Word is living, breathing, moving. It's alive, and yet we often abandon it. We leave it disregarded just when we need it the most. More than merely ignoring it, we actually blaspheme it when we testify opposite of what the Word of God says. Am I sick? Or am I healed? The Word says I'm healed. Am I poor, broken, and destitute? Or am I prosperous, whole, and full of promise? The Word says all of these things and more about me and those under my purview. I cannot reject what God had declared over me and still expect to be well.

Now, as powerful as it is, we have to learn to wield the sword of the Word in righteousness. We cannot use it out of context. We cannot use it against one another. We're on the same team. We have to know when to stand and brace ourselves and when to take that Word and ram it in the gut of the enemy. We can do that. Note, however, that I said *the* enemy, not *we* enemy. We have one adversary: the devil.

Part of this skill is knowing how those of different giftings will use the Word. When a prophet gives you the Word of the Lord, for example, they are not going to sit down and walk you through it. They are not teachers, nor are they always comforters. They are there to declare what God has given them and move on. It's the teacher who will journey with you through the Word.

As we grow in the Word, we will enter seasons when we don't even like to pray with our own words. Instead, we'll declare God's Word from scripture and revelation. We will learn to scout out scriptures and line them up with what is on our hearts, declaring those words as the tree of life. We will also pray in tongues because our own words don't edify the heart of the Father the way that the spiritual language can.

How are we to be victorious? Declare the Word! We may think we have needs, but in truth, the provisions are already in the land. As we declare his promises that say he's already provided for us through what he's given us, we will receive these things.

In 2 Kings 4, Elisha gave oil to a destitute widow, but she already had oil. She just didn't know it. At his command, she prepared empty pots to receive it, and the oil began to flow. She had an abundance of oil.

We have everything we need. It's there. We just have to tap into it through the Word. Our only need is faith in God's Word. He prepared the earth to be everything we would need so that He could dwell in relationship with us.

Please note, however, that God does not provide for our needs so that we can become dependent on spiritual welfare. Yes, there are times when we have nowhere else to go but his daily provision. The Lord sent manna in the wilderness when the Jews had nothing else. But the manna stopped at the Promised Land. Even Jesus fed the multitudes, but only twice. The Lord's goal for us is more than a handout. Our focus is not to be on his hand that provides, but on his face that loves. He's not seeking merely to feed us, but to relate to us. He is a Father who loves his children all the time, not just at mealtime.

Often, and especially as we emerge from poverty, we cannot get past his hand to see his face. Instead, our approach is this: *What's in Your hand, God? What can I have today? What will you give me today? How will you bless me? How will you bring this about? How will you heal me? Restore me? Guide me? Command me?*

The things we seek have already been provided. The blessings are ready. Everything has been given to us, but we have to release it through the power of the Word. We will never learn to handle the Word until we learn what it's for. It's not just to feed us or heal us—yes, those things are vital—but to lead us to the heart of our loving Father. When we realize that the Word is about him, we will know how to wield the sword of the Lord, both in our lives and in the lives of others. We will know love.

Childhood's End

Every answer is found in the Word. If it doesn't come right out and say it in the written Word, God will speak a word directly to you through his Spirit, and you can find the validation in the Bible. You will not be left void. But it is up to each and every one of us to seek out his Word.

There is a difference between seeking God on our own and saying to a teacher, "Well, you're going to have to prove that to me if you expect me to believe it." No, that is not the teacher's role. We've got to get in the Word and search it out ourselves. We can't be spoon-fed the rest of our lives.

At the beginning of this chapter, I quoted the passage from Ecclesiastes which famously declares a time and season for everything. Well, there is a season to be a baby and there is a season to grow up. If you are taking this course, you are in a season to grow up.

Babies and the infirm must be spoon-fed. For the rest of us, our task is seeking out the fresh Word of God so that we can have his life fulfilled within us. The goal is that our very beings can bring about the blessings that God has bestowed on this earth before the foundation of the world.

He gave us the land. He gave us the livelihood. He bought the birthright, and he gave the blessing. It's now up to us to step into these things. Jesus gave his life to restore to us the keys to the kingdom. Now is the time to learn to use them.

If I bring gallons of paint and brushes into my house, does that paint the living room? Of course not. I have to apply it. It's the same with the Word: Apply it! Put it on your doorposts, your mirror, the four corners of your land for protection. Put it on your pillowcases and mattresses for sweet sleep and comforting dreams. Put it under your doormat to welcome strangers. Put it in your vehicle for safe travels and long mechanical life.

Apply the Word to your relationships; teach and admonish one another. The Word, handled in love, supplants gossip, insults, and every form of wickedness. Love, gentleness, kindness, and longsuffering are the foundation of the Word. Everything God does is because of his astounding love for us. As you apply it, let it break forth in songs and hymns and spiritual songs. With grace in your hearts to the Lord, release your sound of adoration to him.

> *Let the message of Christ dwell among you richly as you teach and admonish one another with all wisdom through psalms, hymns, and songs from the Spirit, singing to God with gratitude in your hearts.*

> Colossians 3:16

Since we understand through the Word that he's already made provision for us, we don't have to come before him with a need. Instead, we just declare and decree what is supposed to be, and then we go back and spend intimate time with the Lord.

When we come to a place of intimacy and maturity with him, we become counselors with him. We become the friends of God and we can talk about real matters—things like how the ocean needs to be cleaned up, how the natural resources need to come out of the land, and where that needs to happen to benefit his kingdom. We learn to be strategic, to talk strategies, saying: "OK, Lord, and what do you think about this? How do you think we should approach that?"

And as we grow, he does the same with us.

> *Surely the Sovereign Lord does nothing without revealing his plan to his servants the prophets.*

> Amos 3:7

> *Come now, let us reason together, says the Lord.*

Isaiah 1:18 ESV

The Lord said, "Shall I hide from Abraham what I am about to do, seeing that Abraham shall surely become a great and mighty nation, and all the nations of the earth shall be blessed in him?"

Genesis 18:17-18 ESV

As we develop this deeper relationship with God, our priorities shift. We aren't seeking him for our immediate needs anymore, although we remain thankful for our provision. Rather, we look for direction on higher-order issues such as policy decisions and overall guidance. It's like walking into a board meeting and saying, "We're this much in the red, but we really need to be this much in the black. I'm seeing some wasteful areas, so let's talk about what we should do. Let's talk about where we can give. Let's talk about where we should build. Let's talk about where we should cut back."

As we grow, our dependence on the Word does not diminish. Indeed, it deepens. We need the Word of God because we are all fallible. In fact, if you are not making mistakes, chances are you are not sufficiently challenged. Yes, we all make mistakes and can be misled. This is why scripture tells us:

Do not trust in deceptive words and say, "This is the temple of the Lord, the temple of the Lord, the temple of the Lord!"

Jeremiah 7:4

Many things in this life look good, feel good, cause us to feel special and infuse us with warm fuzzies, but they are not the temple of the Lord. They are not on our side. They may be wearing the same jersey, but they are on the wrong team. The time has come to be "shrewd as snakes and as innocent as doves" (Matthew 10:16). The time has come to know the Word well enough that we can recognize a wolf in sheep's clothing.

And where do we find wolves? Among the flock.

The difficult truth to accept is that there are certain redemptive gifts that fall prey to being victims, and there are other redemptive gifts that fall prey to being predators. The mature among us will recognize the wrong operation of those gifts when we see them. The immature will not. They will live as enablers or worse—as prey.

Baby Battles

I saw a vision once, one that frustrated me and compelled me into intercession. In the vision, I saw these little children coming onto a battleground right in the middle of the battle that I and others were about to fight. The enemy was there, and we were getting ready to charge the enemy when the kids came running in from the side wearing plastic breastplates, colorful helmets and shields. They were cheering, waving foam swords, and pretend-playing about the spiritual things of God.

To be frank, it ticked me off. *What are these kids doing on the battlefield? They're going to get killed. Making matters worse, now we have to divert resources to try to save them.*

The message of the vision was clear: We're not playing anymore. The games are over. The consequences are too great. The price is too steep. Deep is calling unto deep. Iron sharpens iron, but what sharpens us to righteousness is the same weapon that brings the death blow to the enemy. This is not playtime.

We've got to get in the Word. We've got to get into intercession. We've got a war to wage to bring the kingdom of heaven to earth so that our bridegroom may come to his pure and spotless bride.

The war begins at home with the integrity of our lives. When we enter the Ark of the Covenant of the Lord, he sees the innermost parts of us—the good, the bad, the beautiful and the ugly. His inspection reveals everything, especially those areas that we don't see. And know this: When the Lord reveals things about us that need work, we had better get it done because it could cost us our lives. Playtime is over.

Deep calls to deep in the roar of your waterfalls;

all your waves and breakers have swept over me.

Psalm 42:7

If you are going to advance into the deeper things of God, you've got to pay the price. You've got to know the Word. You've got to spend the time in prayer. You've got to seek his face and not his hand. You've got to get beyond your circumstances and realize your identity in Christ Jesus.

We all have our roles to play. It may not be your turn on the battlefield. You might be setting up camp; you might be preparing food; you might be tending to wounds. That's OK. It might be your time to rest, and that's OK as well. But by God, if you think you are a warrior, you'd better know, that you know, that you know that you've been called to that battlefield, because if you show up with your plastic armor and foam sword, you will be destroyed.

This is why we've got to make sure the immature stay off the battlefield. We've got to ensure they're getting their instruction. We all start as children. So let's call it for what it is and not make it something it's not. Some Christians are on the battlefield and others are in nursery school. It's OK to be in nursery school; just don't stay there.

We can't pretend-play anymore . Neither can we be spoon-fed anymore. It's time to work. It's time to go forth in our identities. It's time to start releasing the Word into the lives of people. It's time to teach. It's time to admonish others, building them up and encouraging them to become all that they can be in Christ Jesus. It's our job. It's time to do our job.

> Do not trust in deceptive words and say, "This is the temple of the Lord, the temple of the Lord, the temple of the Lord!"
>
> Jeremiah 7:4

We are in the temple of the Lord. We cannot trust in deceptive words. We are not in the realm of fun and games. Is there a time for laughter? Absolutely. Is there a time for sitting around the table and enjoying one another? Yes, we need that. But when it comes to moving into places of depth with the Lord—when it comes to the righteous seat of judgment or the Ark of the Covenant—these are no places for games. When we say to God, "I lay my life down," we are saying this before a righteous judge. If we are not holy, cleansed and filled with his Word, we will be struck down.

We have to understand our true condition and intentions. The deep things of God require that we enter into his presence with holy fear in extreme trepidation, understanding that he is our righteous judge who sees our hearts. Nothing is hidden from him, not our faults—criticism, deception, strife, division, jealousy, pride and not our positive attributes— charity, love, faithfulness, ardent desire for good and heart-seeking his presence. Our hearts may be hidden from others, but they are not hidden from God.

When we fill ourselves with the Word and marry it with our sounds, life flows, and with it, creativity, love, purity, longsuffering, and patience abounds. Everything within us that is of God is released on earth, bringing his kingdom that his will might be done on earth as it is in heaven. As we walk it out and fulfill it today, Jesus can return to a spotless bride. Not even the hidden parts of her will be corrupt, for "the Spirit searches all things, even the deep things of God" (1 Corinthians 2:10).

Small Beginnings

We can trust God's Word that He will fulfill it as long as we stay faithful and obey. As we walk out our identity, everything around us will be blessed. We will transform our families, our churches, our cities, our nations, and the world.

The early church started out small. Paul was in Asia Minor, and he started building the seven churches one at a time. As each one grew, it so impacted the city that the people threw their idols away and the heathen temple was empty. The occult priests were furious. They rioted in the streets, but still, Paul persisted. In all, over 60,000 people became Christ-ones, and it wasn't going to stop there.

We all begin as Paul began—by releasing the Word. One person saved leads to two, which leads to four. Suddenly, sixteen are reached by the Word, and it spreads exponentially from there.

Our lives sow the Word. Others know us through our actions. They see us for who we are by observing what we do. Hopefully, they're going to see our integrity and become intrigued. They're going to watch how we handle business, treat friends, and manage finances. But mostly, they are going to observe how we love.

Our lives should reflect purity, holiness, and righteousness. It can't be about mental games, manipulation, or control. Forget hidden agendas or trying to build something for yourself. The fruit from our lives, no matter how brief, should be holy, pure and glorify God.

Your name has been established in heaven and on earth. Your name has its own book bearing the things in which you've obeyed. And it has blank pages. Why blank pages? Well, the Lord blots out our sins, but the things in which we don't obey—the things that we don't fulfill—they never are recorded in our book.

What is your land saying about you?

What is your book say about you?

When you stand before the Father, will he say, "Well done, my good and faithful servant"?

Will he gratefully say, "You have released my Word and sown life into my kingdom"?

Will he tell you, "You have made a platform for my Son to come back to behold his virtuous bride"?

Your life doesn't need to look like church. It doesn't need to look like a ministry. But it does need to look like you, and you need to look like Christ.

Sowing the Word

The farmer sows the word.

Mark 4:14

Examine your life by the Spirit. Learn to ask yourself the tough questions that need to be faced.

- What are you sowing?
- What seed are you casting?
- What is the land saying about you?

- Does it edify the Father?
- Does it edify your spirit?
- Does it edify others around you?
- Does it edify your seed?
- Does it edify the family coming into redemption?
- Does it edify the land to yield your provision?
- Does it edify your livelihood so now you can move in your abundance?

As you release your word, you release a sound that either lines up with scripture or doesn't. And when you don't line up with scripture, you are blaspheming the Word of God. You are calling God a liar. The Word is sacred; it must be respected. The enemy is adroit at wielding the Word to trap people in deception. Because of this, we've got to be able to discern when the Word is being used righteously and when it's being used to deceive. When prophecy comes, it may not be laid out in copious amounts of scripture, but if you will get yourself in the Word and seek it out yourself, you will find God will meet you there.

God's Word is enough. In his Word is redemption. In his Word is the blood of Jesus. We disrespect him by not honoring his Word to seek out a thing, neglecting to invest time to find what he has to say about a situation before we release our utterances.

The Word says that I am healed, that my provision is here, that he has provided everything I need through the earth. We don't have to ask what we know to be true. Instead, we declare and decree the answers already because they are found in his promises.

He wants to restore what was in the garden. He wants to restore us as sons and daughters of God. He wants to restore the keys of the kingdom within us to be released in the earth. We have to do it by prophesying his Word. He is the "I Am That I Am." As he is, so are we. As I renew my mind, I renew my spirit. I am in him; he is in me. And no one comes to the Father except through Jesus Christ.

Our identity is to reflect his Word. It was there at creation as a part of the Godhead: Father, Son, Spirit...and Word. "And God said..." (Genesis 1:3).

Consider the power of four. When four winds flow toward each other from opposite directions, they create a convergence that forms a cloud. Now imagine, as we represent the four corners of the earth and we converge in spirit through his Word, that we create a glory cloud of his presence. It's an inverted explosion, a wormhole for the open heavens. The earth opens, the heavens open, and suddenly anything in the middle of that convergence travels through it from earth to heaven and from heaven to earth. Further, everyone hears as they should be because they are in the midst of the convergence.

When Noah shut the door to the ark, it released a sound that called the earth to open up. The earth had not opened up since the garden when it would release water every day to provide for the plants, animals, and mankind. The same thing happened when the ark's door shut—the earth opened up and released the waters. The heavens said, "I agree with you" and it rained. Those waters converged from the four corners of the earth to create a cloud of glory. It was God's protection over the remnant of mankind on the ark, ensuring that they were safely brought through to the other side of his promise. God spoke the promise and then he created the light of his Word through the rainbow.

A Prayer of Repentance

To close this chapter, I suggest this prayer in the spirit of repentance, a spiritual place I go to when faced with my own inadequacies.

Father, I repent for where I have not spoken well of your Word.

I repent for I have spoken against the truths that are established through your Word.

I repent where my testimony has given false testimony of your Word.

I repent, Lord, where my identity was entangled in deception and despair and hopelessness.

I repent that I did not release your Word over my life.

I repent where I didn't release your Word over the situations around me, Lord.

I repent for where I have not reflected your Word well.

I repent, Lord. Your blood, please wash me, purify me.

Make me holy, Lord. Wash me in your Word and put a right spirit within me.

Lord, let this be a new day, a new day of revelation with understanding about the power of your Word, the essential oil, the essential provision, your Word.

Lord, I repent. Forgive me.

Forgive me, O, Lord, where I've dishonored you, where I have just tossed your Word without regard like it's another book and not the treasure trove that it is.

Forgive me for not guarding it the way I would my possessions, my wealth, my children, my livelihood, my seed, Lord, the land.

Forgive me, Lord, for not protecting that holy, precious, precious treasure.

Lord, we thank you that your mercies are new every morning.

Thank You, Lord, that we can change the record of our book by the releasing of your Word, by being obedient to bring your kingdom on earth.

Lord God, fill us with the power of your Word.

Fill us with the might of your Word and teach us how to wield your sword, the Word, well, that it will be wielded correctly, not to harm others on our side, but to use it against the enemy's army and not against one another, that we pick it up and we use it with wisdom. Lord, let us pass this boot camp. Let us come out ready to take the battlefield, ready to take on the enemy, ready to take on new adventures. Let us take back the kingdom through this training. Make us new soldiers, ready to war, ready to do our part. Awaken in us that sleeping giant. Dissolve the slumber that has allowed the Word to just brush by us but not to be consumed within us.

Thank you, Jesus. We bless your name, Lord. You are holy. You are worthy. You are righteous, Lord. Your Word is amen and amen.

12

IDENTITY TO PURPOSE

Arise, shine, for your light has come, and the glory of the Lord rises upon you.

Isaiah 60:1

Sometimes we have to look where we've been to understand our surroundings and the journey we are on. It's easy to get lost. In our burgeoning identity, the weight and responsibilities of life can come in like a flood and cause us to lose sight of who we truly are and what we're intending to do. It doesn't mean there isn't good productivity in the midst of our activities. But we have to remember to go back to the task that we started with, to complete it rather than letting it languish. Such is our identity.

Spiritually, each of us has been assigned the task to rediscover our identity, hence this study. Over the last several chapters, we have been exploring you and who you are. We began by defining what identity actually means. Then we discussed the acquired understanding of who we think we are based on how our needs are met according to Maslow's Hierarchy. We begin to process judgments based on social, or personal responses about what we like, don't like, accept, or don't accept. The process of formulating judgments begins to limit the creative expansion within our identity preventing us from imagining all we can be. These judgments limit our development psychologically, challenging our security, sense of love and belonging, self-esteem, achievement, or respect of others, and forms of self-actualization. Your awakening has begun. What you've been waiting and longing for is here. You are beginning to encounter your personal identity in the fulness of God's glory. This is not who others say you are, but the you who you are created to be. You are made in the image of God to demonstrate his character. This doesn't mean you become someone else, but to become a better version of you through him.

Identity also begins with the development of using our five senses: sight, hearing, taste, smell, and touch. We learn how to operate out of our five senses, not just in physical form, but also in spirit through discernment. It is important to understand the different definitions of identity in order to know whether we made a judgment based on physical, emotional, or social influences, because we are affected by things around us. Yes, external things influence how we move and operate, but do they identify us? No, they don't. When using our senses, we make certain choices in the natural, but we also tap into the spirit as Christ leads us.

This is important because our judgments or choices determine how we engage with one another. My choices will affect the people around me and the vast numbers of unknown people, and their choices affect me. We affect one another through what is referred to as the Law of Entanglement. The Law of Entanglement is used in quantum physics saying relationship is a defining characteristic of all things in time and space. For instance, think of the way that atoms interact in relation to one another. Relationship doesn't require a physical link, yet all things are connected in space. Therefore, all creation is in relationship due to the Law of Entanglement. Moreover, we are not just physical beings but also spiritual beings. The scripture in Romans 12:5, refers to us as one body being many parts. These laws not only engage us with one another, spirit to spirit, but they also engage us with the land and what it produces. They affect other things as well, such as our professions, education, and our beliefs about family and tradition. All of those things are blended through Laws of Entanglement which are inasmuch affected by our choices. When we choose to expand our identity in obedience and love, it has a monumental impact.

Spiritual Integrity

When addressing our spiritual integrity, we have to assess whether we still have emotional wounds, perhaps hidden ones that go back years. Further, we need to uncover why they are there and not getting any better.

This starts with discovering the open doors that happened because of willful sin or sins of ignorance. There are typically four doors that affect our identity: Fear/Believing a Lie, Unforgiveness, Sexual Sins, and the Occult. Most sins will fall into one of these four categories. Religion may tell you what sin is but search out the Word, so you may know for yourself. In addition, there may not be something written in the scripture, but Holy Spirit may convict you about something. This becomes a personal conviction for you but does not mean that you rule others by it. Holy Spirit gives us wisdom with revelation and understanding. Let him guide you to knowledge.

The doors are opened through willful sins or sins of ignorance. Willful sins are those sins which you do out of rebellion and disobedience. Sins of ignorance may be done without your full knowledge or understanding that it was wrong. This is why we need to know what scripture says is a sin.

Inner Healing

There are several demonic spirits that can oppress us. Say someone constantly struggles with rejection. That person lives under a spirit of rejection. They are going to walk out relationships and decisions through a filter of rejection. This is the reason we should all work to get emotional wounds healed, so we can walk in the prosperity of the kingdom message that says we are healed and not rejected. Indeed, we are received under the blood of Jesus and made new. We are adopted into kingdom relationship. We no longer live for ourselves. We are now part of the collective body of Christ. I am no longer rejected and isolated. Just because I may be a pinky on the body of God, I'm still part of the whole entity. My job as a pinky is just as valuable as any other part.

Our inner healing starts through repentance. We repent for those thoughts and beliefs that allowed our wounds to occur and fester. We repent for judgments that we may have made, and we begin to bring healing to our wounded emotions through God's Word. As we do that, the fruits of the spirit manifest within us and we begin to grow in redemption.

Our words—our sound, as we studied earlier—control the power of life and death. If I speak negatively to a plant, it begins to shrivel and wilt. Now, imagine what your spirit does under rejection, bitterness, pride, or anger. It begins to shrivel. It's dying. In marriage, if a husband talks down to his wife and insults her, especially in front of people, making her feel small, her spirit shuts down and she begins to withhold love. She doesn't have to say anything, but it happens within her and manifests outwardly. It is communicated through her actions, such as when she can no longer enjoy the pleasure of her husband and begins to push him away, building a wall and blocking their intimacy. There's something corrosive between them: hurt, rejection, and embarrassment. It could be any or all of those things. But when he speaks kindness to her, when he elevates her publicly, when he adores her privately, her spirit begins to flourish again.

The same is true with the words we speak over our own lives. When we speak God's Word, our spirit begins to open up and our identity firms up. We're not closed off anymore. Rather, we are open to receive the fullness of relationship, both with God and with people, because we're not walking in those things as a closed being anymore.

Our spiritual integrity is at the root of our being. If our spirit man is not healed, it affects everything else about us. It affects us physically and mentally. It affects our relationships. It affects the things that are designed to prosper us. We have to maintain spiritual integrity, to open doors that need to be opened to the kingdom and close doors to the enemy that give him access to our lives.

The purpose for open doors and open gates is for us to move freely in our identity in Jesus Christ, to receive all of the gifts of the kingdom and operate effectively and efficiently through them to benefit those around us as well as ourselves, bringing the kingdom of heaven right here on earth.

Resolving Conflict

As part of the process of inner healing, we transition through conflict. Nobody likes conflict, yet as long as we're in relationship, we are going to experience conflict. We're going to have conflicts of time, business, marital and parental, to name a few. It's a part of our nature because we're human beings.

In Christ, we learn how to move through conflict in a healthy manner, how to communicate effectively, to voice our concerns and needs. Meanwhile, we validate others and allow them to voice their concerns and needs. In managing our conflict, we need to care for ourselves and others.

If we are in a relationship, we need to value the relationship even when we're called to separate ourselves from it. We're not bridge burners; we're bridge builders. Now, granted, we're not always given that choice. It takes two to make a relationship. But we, as redeemed men and women, have to create the passage from our end so that others can come meet us in that place of reconciliation at any time.

This is not always easy. In my life, there are many times that I prefer to walk away or just disappear, but I have accountability with my Father. He is watching everything, not just what others see of me, but the things that I know behind closed doors—the things that I utter to him and him alone. He's watching me to see that I will move well in difficult relationships because, if I can be trusted in the relational things of God, he will bring me to even greater things.

If we can learn how to communicate effectively, to forgive and forget, then we can be trusted to do what Jesus says in Matthew 18—to reconcile with others and make room for restoration.

Difficult situations may come and go, but their emotional effects don't go as easily. There have been situations that played over and over in my mind until I thought, "Oh dear God, it would have been easier if I had just been killed."

Of the trials and tribulations that you go through on this earth, only you know their depth and reach. That is your pain and your pain alone. Often, whoever hurt you doesn't know; sometimes, they don't even care. In the final analysis, your pain and damage are between you and God.

What are your choices? You can go through life injured and bitter. Nobody would know except you. But it will affect everything you do because, in the back of your mind, you're waiting for the other shoe to drop. *When is somebody else going to come along and hurt me? When is someone else going to do this thing? Is this person a good one or...?*

And it starts all over again.

But every time you overcome that difficult place, it becomes easier. Once you've overcome something, you now have become a victorious warrior in that area. The benefit, other than your own healing, is that you get to help someone else through the same situation. So, the difficult situation wasn't for loss. It was for your growth.

Reconcile and Forgive

Communication, compromise, accommodation, avoidance, and collaboration are the tools we use to reconcile. The other people involved may not be ready, but as a mature Christ-one, it's incumbent upon us to be ready when they are finally ready. We do this by being prepared within and without.

We have to be ready to reconcile. We have to be ready even though it's not the most comfortable place to be in. Jesus was not in a comfortable place when He was being accused. When everyone was crying *blasphemy*, he stayed true to his message.

> *But you don't understand. If you all go back to Isaiah, I'm quoting to you the very words that prophesied my coming. I'm saying to you, I'm showing you, I'm revealing to you. My Father even gave his spoken word and there were witnesses there. They testified of me. My Father spoke to me. The whole spirit descended as a dove unto me, and this is being fulfilled. If you will turn from your wicked ways. If you will believe me and hear the words that I'm saying to you. There is a kingdom realm that is coming on to you. It is here in the midst of you. Partake of me, be part of me.*

It wasn't easy for him to do that. It wasn't easy for him to choose his 12 disciples, knowing ahead of time that one would betray him, another would deny him, and most would not fully get his message for a long time. He knew it, but he worked with them anyway, and all but one repented and carried the kingdom message to the world.

There will be times when we have to work with people even though we see the potential for pain. We must learn to stand to make the possible damages as minimal as possible. We have an enemy, and this enemy seeks to destroy all that God is doing. There will be people sent to you to destroy you because you represent the kingdom of God. The people may not even know what they're doing. The teachers who cried *blasphemy* in Jesus' face didn't know whom they were accusing. When they crucified Jesus, they didn't understand. Even Jesus said, "Father, forgive them, for they do not know what they are doing" (Luke 23:34).

The same is true of most people. They don't know. They're operating out of places of their own personal woundedness which has opened doors to be an instrument for the enemy, and they don't even know it. So how can you blame them? I have made mistakes and God allowed grace for me. Not only did he forgive me but he allowed others to forgive me and my woundedness. There are times I act out. I say something through fatigue and wounds, statements that don't come out in a healthy state of mind. I trust that others will forgive me as freely as I forgive them. My measure is in no way equal to that of the Father's or to what Jesus paid for forgiveness, but I must follow his example, forgiving where I need to and seeking forgiveness when I was at fault.

Forgiveness is part of our spiritual integrity. If we do not forgive our brother, then Jesus cannot freely forgive us. I want his mercy. I want this grace. I want to be free to operate and move. I want to be trustworthy. He trusts me with others. He trusts me to do the will that he has placed within me. Yet, if I cannot forgive my brothers and sisters in Christ, I'm not effective in fulfilling the call that has been set before me.

Abrahamic Blessings

Through our ancestral identifiers, we tap into the things that come from the blessing of Abraham. These were established with Adam in the garden. God's plan was this: *I'm going to provide the seed through Abraham to bring about my son. I will establish this covenant with Abraham now, so that when my son comes, all he has to do is go back and take the keys.*

Jesus restored to us the covenant that God made with Abraham.

God created Adam for relationship. Our identity, everything that we are, is about relationship—our relationship with Christ and with others. Jesus was the example. He paid the ultimate price for relationship. He demonstrated and walked it out well. Now it is up to us to complete it to bring his kingdom to the earth.

The seed that is us, our DNA, contains those generational things that began with Adam. They were later reestablished with Abraham, and finally were fulfilled through Jesus Christ. Now we reestablish that kingdom as he gave us the keys. *Now I've made you manager of the field. Go and tend to it.*

So now we break things off of our generational line all the way back to Adam, and we released new things on our generational line. We are the conduit that restores the past and brings about the future. We hold the keys, just as Jesus restored it all. He said, "Do not think that I have come to abolish the Law or the Prophets; I have not come to abolish them but to fulfill them" (Matthew 5:17). He did that so we could regain what had been lost with Adam, and it comes through our seed. It is our family line. Everything begins with family.

Spiritual Identity

That breath of God, that creative fire that first brought life to man, is now residing in us. It comes out through our spiritual identity to present itself before God. It is that breastplate that goes before God. It is that place where we say: "Here we are, Lord God. This is our spirit that has been reestablished."

Our flesh is hidden behind that breastplate that we now call righteousness because of our historical identifiers. It was the tribe, the son, and the seed that came out of Abraham through Jacob that established the tribes and the rule that was the 12 stones. And not only the 12 stones, but also as the 12 disciples of God to go into the earth and reestablish God's kingdom on earth.

We are kings and priests. We work in partnership with the land because in the beginning, God created the land to be our resource. We were to subdue it and take dominion. So, from the land, God established relationship with Adam and Eve. They didn't come to Him wondering: *Where is our food coming from?* His answer was all around him: *I've created everything here for you to it. The animals can eat of it. There's nothing that you have need of that I've not provided right here.*

God provided for all their needs in the garden. There was safety and physiological balances, and their self-actualization was the glory of God—God's very presence. They understood that they were the sons and daughters of God.

As kings and priests, we understand that we come before God as priests for atonement of our sins. Yet we have the rule and the scepter in our hands to rule and establish dominion on behalf of our Savior and Lord. When he returns, he will establish his throne. We are co-heirs with Jesus, so we have rule and dominion with him.

> *Now if we are children, then we are heirs—heirs of God and co-heirs with Christ, if indeed we share in his sufferings in order that we may also share in his glory.*

> Romans 8:17

Through this blood relationship, he gave us the five governmental gifts that come through salvation: Apostles, Prophets, Evangelists, Pastors and Teachers. Five is also the number of grace, so we know that these gifts are established through grace. That is our governmental rule. He can't trust the wicked with it. It can only come through Jesus Christ. Only the righteous can have dominion with God, and they are trusted with the five keys.

This includes the birthright. We go back through the womb under the blood of Jesus. That atonement creates a new birth and a new identity that gives us the birthright that Adam had and lost. It is restored through Jesus

Christ. Coming to that new birthright brings us to the seed and the land. Through the seed and the land, the blessing of abundance comes through the Father. We have our new identity established. We're beginning to fulfill that process on earth. We are made new. Our love is our blessing.

Spiritual Integrity

In the Old Testament, Jacob went to work for Laban because he fell in love with Laban's daughter, Rachel. But instead of marrying her, he was tricked by Laban into marrying her sister, Leah. A week later he married Rachel and had to work another seven years for her. As he worked, the favor of God was upon him. Yet, he had not gained anything for himself other than his wives. Laban was prospering, but not Jacob. Finally, Jacob said to Laban, "Since you have prospered, let me have some of this wage." From then on, everything Jacob did was blessed in Jacob's favor even though his father-in-law had done him wrong.

Jacob's story shows us that it doesn't matter what people do to you. It can hurt your feelings, hurt your bank account, hurt your family, but in the long run, they are not making an eternal impact on your life unless you choose to let them. Indeed, when God sees you operate well in spite of the misguided judgments of others, the blessing of abundance will be poured out upon you. It can't help but happen because it's the very nature of God. That has an eternal impact because not only does your life change from your choices, but your generational line is transformed.

Stand righteously in the Word of God; bind and loose according to Jesus' teaching: "Truly I tell you, whatever you bind on earth will be bound in heaven, and whatever you loose on earth will be loosed in heaven" (Matthew 18:18).

Bless those who use you. Bind good things to them. Bind that spiritual wickedness that's been affecting them. Operate out of love, and loose blessings upon them so that they receive a reward in spite of their behavior. "Bless those who curse you, pray for those who mistreat you" (Luke 6:28). There's a reward and abundant blessing that comes through this action. It changes your eternal destination, not just salvation and forgiveness, but the tangible components that reshape your generational line.

When your spiritual integrity is transposed to the generations, you are establishing a kingdom of God that cannot be assailed. My children have seen me walk through conflicts that have shaped their lives. Now they see the blessings that have come as a product of the choices I made in the midst of the struggle. The battle may have been mine but now that it's won, it doesn't have to be theirs. They can easily walk through new territory because they've seen it demonstrated. They know what the right thing is, and they can walk in it. It's become part of their identity. They've seen it demonstrated time and time again, so they don't have to make a conscious choice. It's a part of their identity now and will remain so for generations.

This is how we transform our region and nation. The actions that I choose to make today impact my children, my children's children and so on. If I will pay the price today, they won't have to do the same in the generations to come. Instead, they will be revolutionizing, transforming, bringing about new changes not possible in my generation. Indeed, the challenges that they will face will be altogether new.

My children are walking through new forms of identity and shaping their children's identity. As they continue to walk out God's Word, this thing that has not changed since the beginning of time with no beginning and no end...as they walk in this scripture that proves itself, they are transforming everything. It's a ripple. This is how we change the world, and it starts in the decisions that we make today.

Consider where your circle of influence is today. Because no matter where it is now, it is going to be greater five years from now. Your sound is being transferred through your DNA. We go back to God's sound, that resolute sovereign sound of the Word that brought all things into existence, that which survives the ages and will never pass away.

Our Identity

So, who are we?

In the beginning, we had all these things to consider about our natural identity: skills, traits, even shoe size. Yes, we are all that, but we are so much more. When we start stepping into our historical and messianic identity, heaven and earth become ours.

Our sound should be full of God's Word because in the Word is his identity. Our identity reflects his identity. As I release the sound, his Word should be released. It is for the edification of one another. We have the Word to understand his identity through relationship. We remain in relationship with him while we edify one another in his Word. Teachers may not have the right words for you, but God's Word certainly does.

There's much to the name of the Lord, so much so that we can sometimes take it for granted. Our identity is in our names, but it's also in his name. It's one thing to say: "Oh, I'm Tom's daughter." But it's entirely different to say: "I'm Elohim's daughter." The first gives me definition in my family and my region. But the second opens doors in the spirit that I may not be able to open on my own. In my flesh, I have no strength, no might, but in my identity in him there is no door closed to me that I cannot open, and no door open that I cannot shut.

> *I will place on his [Jesus's] shoulder the key to the house of David; what he opens no one can shut, and what he shuts no one can open.*

> Isaiah 22:22

I am in him. He is in me.

We should use the Lord's name more often when we identify ourselves. I am victorious. I am loved. It's a reflection of my Father in heaven when I say who I am. I cannot separate the two anymore. People wonder why they're lost, hungry, possessed of a void that cannot be filled. It's because they use God's name and don't even understand that their identity is in him. It injures their spirit when they say anything contrary to the Word of God. It builds a wall, shutting down their spirit as they begin to close themselves off. They're hurting themselves and they don't know it. Worse, they're hurting that truth about their Father. Remember, God is good. The enemy is bad. God is love. When we come through the blood of Jesus, our eyes are opened to see his goodness. We taste his loving-kindnesses. Our spirit is opened because we now acknowledge his identity. We understand that his intent is not to hurt us but to do good for us.

I hope that through this study, you have a better understanding of your identity, although we've only scraped the surface of knowledge and experience. There's more. Can you believe it? There's so much more.

We can't step into the fullness of our identity without having some work done. We are here to subdue and rule in dominion. The choices that we make have an eternal impact that will be seen on earth and documented in heaven. Whatever's done on earth has to manifest in heaven, and whatever happens in heaven must manifest on earth. It's the law of the kingdom. When you don't immediately see the things you want, don't give up, because it's here. It's here and so are you. You are the conduit to bring those things from kingdom to kingdom. When you transfer from earth to heaven, heaven will come into agreement with you and send it in the perfection of God. Then it's released back into the earth.

We all have whys, and God knows the answers. It comes down to our purpose. Even though each individual has a purpose, and every person's purpose moves through times and seasons and may not always look the same, we, the body of Christ, have an overlying purpose that continues to be the same for everyone throughout all eternity—relationship.

To find out more about your specific purpose that coordinates with Father's, read *Purpose: The Destiny Series.*

Daily Prayer

> *Thank you, Lord, for assisting me through this exploration of my identity that incorporates your precepts. I receive my complete healing and restoration of who you created me to be. I am eternally grateful for this day.* 😊

CONGRATULATIONS!! YOU FINISHED!!

ABOUT THE AUTHOR

Rebecca Bennett and her husband, Crispin, are the founders of Wells of SouthGate, based in Mississippi. Their vision includes an apostolic hub across the Gulf Coast for the training and equipping of the ekklesia in this new era: "Out of Error," where operating in the fivefold gifts is not only taught but demonstrated and discipled. Through the School of Ministry, believers become more effective within every sphere of influence.

Rebecca's passion is to show people how to live in the fulness of all life has to offer. Wells of SouthGate has a community-minded focus for basic life skills, education, leadership training, job placement, business planning, home-buying strategies, and finance. It presently partners with several ministries and is affiliated with Network Ecclesia International (NEI).

Since her teens, Rebecca has honed skills as an entrepreneur. In 1994, she became the owner/operator of B&B Enterprises where the primary focus has been Real Estate Investments. Businesses birthed out of B&B Enterprises operate in the Kingdom Principles and core values that Rebecca teaches in this series. Because of their success, she can spend more time teaching others.

It was late September in 2017, when a download of thoughts came funneling through Rebecca's mind. As she jotted them down, they became separated into four sections. After a few weeks of contemplation, they became Identity, Purpose, Authority and Leadership, what is now _The Destiny Series._ It is a journey of education, experience, and hope; one that she longs to take you on, to the glory of God.

Rebecca is available for speaking and teaching engagements, and can be reached at
rebeccadbennett.tds@gmail.com

~

Visit her website at

www.rebeccadbennett.com.

www.kligulfcoast.com or www.wellsofsouthgate.com

The Destiny Series Books

STRATEGIC TRAINING TO DISCOVER YOU

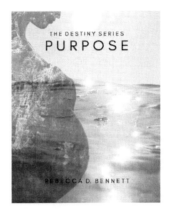

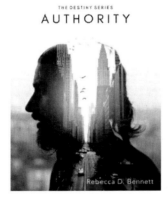

The Destiny Series is designed to help you discover the who and the why that you are. You are designed to become a great leader that God intended you to be, and you can reach your maximum potential in the ministry that the Lord Jesus gave every person (Matthew 28:19).

This dynamic and interactive series is available for individual or group study, as well as an author led course. To learn more, visit **www.rebeccadbennett.com or www.kligulfcoast.org.**

A Publishing Assist Company
Honor & Excellence as the seedbed of your written work

3Trees Publishing was born the result of the architectural build out of Wells of SouthGate. Following the blueprints for the region, 3Trees Publishing serves to reconnect creatives with their kingdom calling by supplying a framework of excellence for all printed work. This endeavor reintroduces and reconstitutes the original intent and design for the Spanish West Florida Territory and beyond. Let the expression of your purpose be revealed as you prepare legacy for those who come after. For more information, contact us at **3treespublishing@gmail.com.**

Doors, Gates, and Thresholds Series

THE NAME Speaks

ANGELA BROUSSARD

THE NAME Speaks by Angela Broussard
His sound reverberates. Can you hear Him speak your name?

It is said that life is a journey and we are pilgrims on it. Discovering our strengths, weaknesses and opponents on the journey exposes the reality of the spiritual realm - and just how fortified it is. Each installment of Doors, Gates, and Thresholds will equip you to successfully navigate the unseen structural components of both the Kingdom of God and the Kingdom of darkness, leading you to victory upon victory. This, in turn, will empower the corporate expression of the Ekklesia, releasing power in greater measure, and you bring your victory to bear upon the whole.

The Name Speaks is the introduction to the Master Poet and His creation: you. Engage in the formation of your identity within the large context of the Kingdom, and come to know your vital role in service to the King. For more information visit: www.silvercornerstone.com or www.kligulfcoast.org.

Designs x Laura
Let's manifest your vision

Designs x Laura is a brand and service for helping others find and interpret their vision. Whether you offer a product or service, are new or established in your field or maybe don't know what the next step is for you, you're covered!

For web design, graphic design and marketing services, please visit www.designsxlaura.com or email contact@designsxlaura.com for a free consultation. If you don't see a specific need listed, feel free to reach out and our team will be happy to assist and discuss the innovation of your ideas.

Education

MAKING EXCELLENCE VISIBLE

KLI GULF COAST

The leadership institute of choice prepares you for leadership in the Kingdom of God. The strategy of KLI Gulf Coast is individualized. Your leadership training can begin at any level of spiritual and ministry maturity. We start where you are with what you do. As one can function in any aspect of culture, once taught to function in kingdom culture, the Institute educates and prepares students for any arena of occupation. We honor kingdom leaders from every walk of life. Students come from many professions and occupations.

Partnered with KLI Jacksonville, our course intensives develop mature individuals to impact the current culture with Kingdom culture. Determine today to engage your life's work at the starting gate of Kingdom Leadership Institute Gulf Coast. For more information, or to enroll, visit www.kligulfcoast.org or contact us at kligulfcoast@gmail.com.

Wells of SouthGate
Serve * Train* Empower

- Community Advancement
- Business Training
- Leadership Development

We Bring The Trainer To You.

Call today to discuss and implement the strategic training that's best for your business or field of influence!

838 Howard Ave
Biloxi, MS 39532

228-331-0017

www.wellsofsouthgate.com

Wells of SouthGate is a training, equipping, and activating center on the Mississippi Gulf Coast. Our passion is to see each person matured to fulfill our God-given dreams and destiny, to become a flourishing, contributing member of their society. For more information, visit our website: **www.wellsofsouthgate.com.**

Made in United States
North Haven, CT
26 October 2022

25917514R00102